Contents

	1698	1699	1700	1701	1702
West strip field	Wheat	Barley	Fallow	Wheat	Barley
South strip field	Barley	Fallow	Wheat	Barley	Fallow
East strip field	Fallow	Wheat	Barley	Fallow	Wheat
Years	1698	1699	1700	1701	1702

England in about 1700

What was life and work like about this time?

In the villages, where four out of five people lived, life on the land continued to follow the customs and traditions laid down in Norman times.

Using the same primitive tools, most families lived at subsistence level, producing sufficient for their own needs and perhaps some surplus to sell in nearby market-towns.

The vicar of the parish still collected his tithe, the church tax. The tenth sucking-pig might end up on his table, the tenth sheaf of corn in his barn. The vicar and the lord of the manor were usually the chief landowners in the village. They expected to see their tenant farmers and labourers at church every Sunday.

▲ A harvest celebration

Harvesting, which took place every August, still dominated the country calendar. A good harvest was always celebrated. If it was poor, the consequences were cruel. Wet weather ruined crops, sheep died of liver-rot and cattle caught foot-and-mouth disease. Hay-ricks went mouldy and corn-stacks were not worth threshing.

In order to grow more corn, improvements such as draining marshes and fenland had been made. Some farmers copied a Dutch idea of a four-course rotation. Instead of leaving one field fallow, as was the general practice in England, they grew turnips, which were good animal fodder, and clover, which enriched the soil.

Many farmers at this time had never seen a turnip, and continued to cultivate their various strips of land in the open-field system, now centuries old.

▲ Farming methods in 1700 – unchanged for hundreds of years

QUEST

The World of Empire, Industry and Trade

Bea Stimpson

Stanley Thornes (Publishers) Ltd

First published in 2000 by:
Stanley Thornes (Publishers) Ltd
Ellenborough House
Wellington Street
CHELTENHAM GL50 IYW
England

00 01 02 03 04 / 10 9 8 7 6 5 4 3 2 1

A catalogue record for this book is available from the British Library.

ISBN 0-7487-3660-3

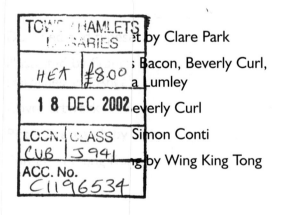

... t by Clare Park

... Bacon, Beverly Curl,
... Lumley

... everly Curl

... Simon Conti

... by Wing King Tong

The author wishes to acknowledge Peter Burton and Barry Page of Stanley Thornes for their advice during the preparation of this book.

Thanks are owed to the illustrators for their skill and patience in producing the artwork. She also wishes to thank her teaching colleague Alan Coulson for his practical suggestions.

She is particularly indebted to her husband, Michael, for the support he has given.

Acknowledgements

With thanks to the following for permission to reproduce photographs and illustrations:

Bedfordshire & Luton Archives and Records Service: 33(t)

Birmingham Museums and Art Gallery: 104(r), 114(t)

Bridgeman Art Library: (Bibliotheque Nationale, Paris) 54(r), (Blenheim Palace) 12(b), (Guildhall Library, Corporation of London) 89(b), (Leeds Museums and Galleries, Lotheron Hall) 55(b), (National Gallery, London) 101(b), (Portsmouth City Art Gallery) 124(b), (Yale Center for British Art, Paul Mellon Collection) 34(b)

Bristol Museums: 64(l)

City of Manchester Art Gallery: 114(b)

Communist Party Picture Library: 77(b), 92(t)

The Co-operative Union Ltd: 94(t), 94(b)

E.T.Archive: 16(c), 58(b), 80(b), 123(t)

The Fotomas Index: 6(c), 18(t), 21(t), 31(b), 37(b), 40(b), 58(t), 64(r), 73(r)

Getty Images: 31(t), 41(b), 65(b), 83(b), 88(b), 95(t), 120(r)

The Ironbridge Gorge Museum Trust: 7(b), 52(t), 112(b)

Kirklees Community History Service: 5(b)

The Maritime Trust: 100(b)

Mary Evans Picture Library: 5(t), 21(b), 23(l), 29(t), 34(t), 35(t), 35(b), 38(t), 39(r), 41(t), 43(b), 46(b), 47(t), 47(b), 50(b), 56(t), 62(b), 63(t), 66(b), 68(b), (Bruce Castle Museum) 70(b), 72(t), 75(b), 81(b), 82(b), 86(t), 86(b), 93(b), 96(b), 97(b), 98(t), 102(b), 103(b), 104(l), 105(t), 105(b), 106(t), 106(b), 107(r), 108(t), 110(b), 113(t), 113(b), 115(r), 117(b), 119(b), 121(t), 121(b), 123(b)

Merthyr Tydfil County Borough Council, Cyfartha Castle: 53(b)

Courtesy of the Museum of the Lancashire Textile Industry, Helmshore, Lancashire: 39(l)

Courtesy of the Director, National Army Museum, London: 117(t)

National Library of Australia: 67(b)

National Maritime Museum London: 57(b), 99(t), 99(b), 100(t)

By Courtesy of the National Portrait Gallery, London: 10(t), 13(t), 14(t), 19(t), 78(b)

National Waterways Archive, Gloucester: 45(b)

Newport Museum: 91(b)

Reproduced by permission of the Palace of Westminster: 11(c), 14(b)

Peter Newark's Pictures: 24(t), 24(b), 25(t), 26(b), 27(b), 54(l)

The Royal Collection © Her Majesty The Queen: 15(b), 28(t), 76(l), 93(t)

Philip Sauvain: 111(t), 111(b)

Science & Society Picture Library: 8(r), 29(b), 38(b), 40(t), 48(l), 48(r), 51(t), 51(b), 52(b), 70(t), 71(t), 71(b), 72(b)

The Trustees of Sir John Soane's Museum: 76(r)

V & A Picture Library, Victoria & Albert Museum, London: 59(b), 74(t)

Trustees of the Wedgwood Museum Limited: 42(t), 42(b), 44(t)

The Wellcome Trust Medical Photographic Library: 109(t), 109(b)

Every effort has been made to contact copyright holders and we apologise if any have been inadvertently overlooked.

Preparatory	Spinning	Weaving	Finishing	
Sorted into grades Scoured Washed and dried Carded through wire teeth Some dyeing	Sliver of thread drawn out and twisted for strength	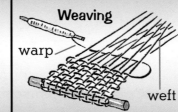 warp / weft	Scouring in fulling stocks Washing and dyeing Stretching and drying Tentering (on tenterhooks) Shearing	Teasels for raising nap 

Woollen cloth production

Cottage industries

What other work was there in the village?

England's second main industry was the wool trade, and families could supplement their meagre earnings by helping to produce woollen cloth.

▲ Carding combs and spinning-wheels

Every cottage would have its spinning-wheel. Children were taught how to clean and card the raw material; women and children did the spinning; and the more strenuous weaving was done by men at hand-looms. When the woollen cloth was taken off the loom, it still had to be washed, cleaned, bleached and dyed. This was done in workshops attached to cottages or in larger workshops in towns.

Some cloths, such as soft velvet, had to have the nap raised with teasels. Finally the cloth was cropped – clipped with shears to give it a regular surface.

Who organised this trade?

The wealthy merchant 'clothiers' bought the wool and supervised every stage of manufacture. A 'middleman' would bring the raw wool by packhorse and collect the woollen cloth to be finished elsewhere if necessary.

Other workshops specialising in various trades were also attached to cottages. These domestic industries such as nail-making, glass-blowing, pottery and brick-making, would involve whole families.

Villages with their blacksmith, carpenter, thatcher and miller were largely self-sufficient. Other trades – the butcher, the baker, the candlestick-maker – were carried on in small towns so that most needs were met locally. People tended not to travel far.

▲ Hand-raising and shearing in the cropper's workshop

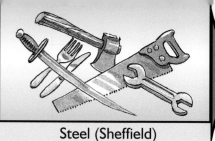

The iron and steel industry

Everyone in villages and towns needed iron and steel goods – fire-grates, cutters for ploughs, cutlery, tools and so forth.

How was iron and steel made?

Basically, from the same process – smelting (melting) iron ore.

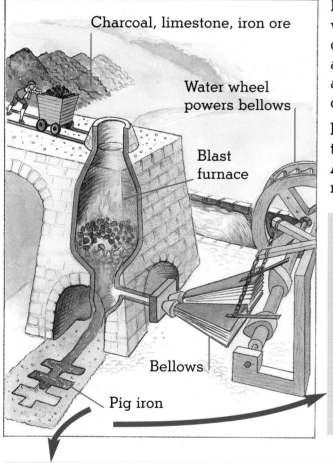

Charcoal, limestone, iron ore

Water wheel powers bellows

Blast furnace

Bellows

Pig iron

Iron ore, a reddish-brown earthy material, was mined. It was mixed with limestone from quarries and charcoal from coppicewood to help remove impurities. It was poured into a furnace where charcoal had been burning for several days at 1400° C. Heavy molten (melted) iron sank through the charcoal into 'pigs', rectangular sandy moulds.

Furnaces had to be sited near limestone quarries. There had to be running water for water power to work the bellows. And there had to be woodlands: it took an acre of timber to make sufficient charcoal to make two tonnes of pig iron.

Wrought iron

The pig iron could be re-heated and hammered with a tilt-hammer to drive out impurities. It was shaped by rollers into bars, sheets or rods, then made into smaller items such as locks, bolts and buttons.

▲ A traditional nail-making forge

Cast iron

The pig iron could be ladled straight into moulds to make pots and pans.

Steel

To make steel, cast iron had to be refined and 7% carbon added. Iron bars and charcoal (pure carbon) would be heated together in clay pots. It took nearly three weeks to produce ten tonnes of 'blister steel' of uneven quality. This was used for scissors, files and other tools.

By 1720 there were only about sixty blast furnaces in England. There were huge deposits of iron ore and ample running water, but supplies of timber were scarce.

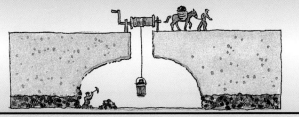
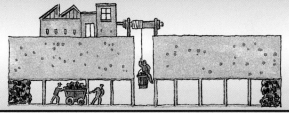
Coke and coal

Trees had been felled not just for charcoal, but for shipbuilding, machines and general use. To meet the ever-increasing demand for iron goods, Britain had to import pig and bar iron from Russia and Sweden.

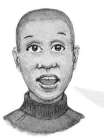

Why wasn't coal used as fuel?

It was, in industries such as brick-making, but when it was used in smelting, its sulphur compounds ruined the iron, making it brittle and unworkable.

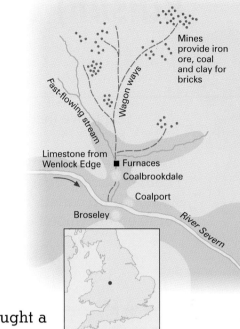

Mines provide iron ore, coal and clay for bricks

Fast-flowing stream

Wagon ways

Limestone from Wenlock Edge ■ Furnaces
Coalbrookdale

Coalport

Broseley

River Severn

▲ Site of Coalbrookdale

The solution was found by Abraham Darby who, in 1708, bought a disused ironworks in Coalbrookdale, Shropshire. He had observed that the malt industry used coke (pit coal without sulphur) and experimented with this. In 1709 he produced coke-smelted pig iron which, though not suitable for wrought iron, was ideal for his pots and pans. These were exported all over the world.

blast furnaces

heavy casting pulled by team of horses

wagon on railway coming down incline

furnace pool provided water for water-powered bellows

coal burnt to coke in heaps

▲ Coalbrookdale

As the demand for coke for use in blast furnaces increased, ironworks were built on coal fields and good transport routes. Coalbrookdale was well situated: near to coal, iron and clay mines, limestone quarries and the River Severn. Horses brought coal to Darby's works from the nearby mine at Broseley by pulling laden chaldrons (trucks) along wooden rails.

A horse-drawn jenny (engine) was used to haul men and coal to the surface in baskets on ropes. Work in mines was gloomy, grimy and dangerous.

Raising water by fire

What were the dangers in early coal mines?

Explosive methane gas, light and safety, ventilation and flooding.

The problem of flooding was tackled as early as 1698 by steam power. Captain Thomas Savery developed the work of a French scientist, Denis Papin, to produce a steam pump called 'the Miner's Friend'. This could raise water for over ten metres, but used enormous amounts of coal and was liable to explode.

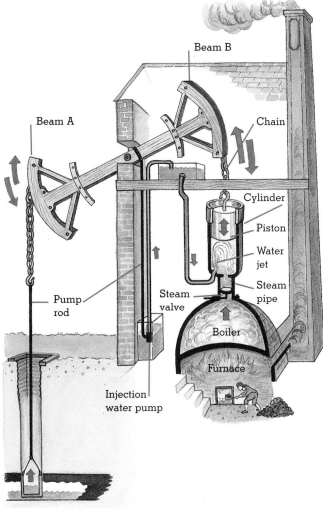

Savery went into partnership with a blacksmith and locksmith, Thomas Newcomen. The next 'Engine to Raise Water by Fire' worked rather like a see-saw:

- Water in the boiler is heated by the fire and turns into steam

- Steam enters cylinder through a valve and cannot return into boiler

- When steam fills cylinder it is condensed (changed back into water) into a smaller space by a jet of cold water

- This causes a vacuum under the piston

- Atmospheric pressure from above the piston forces it down to bottom of cylinder

- Beam B moves down

- Beam A moves up and the bucket at the end of the pump-rod lifts water out of the mine

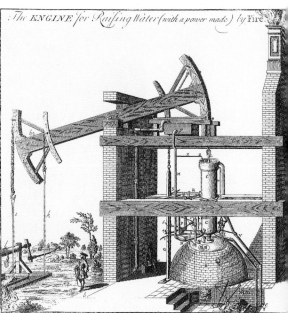

▲ Newcomen's steam engine, 1711

Newcomen's engine pumped water from a depth of over 100 metres and used less coal (13 tonnes a day). It was noisy but reliable, and became popular for use in mines for over 60 years. In 1742 Abraham Darby's son installed one at Coalbrookdale to raise water to drive the wheel for the blast furnaces.

Transport

Demand for industrial coal increased, but because of transport difficulties, most was still used in or near mining areas for domestic fires. London, not sited near a coalfield, was supplied with coal from Tyneside.

How was the coal transported?

By sea. London also received corn from Sussex and Hampshire, and cheese from Cheshire by sea.

Despite the risk of salt water spoiling goods, and attacks by privateers, sea transport was cheaper and preferable to river and road transport. Rivers were often too shallow and crossed by low bridges.

Improvements were made to the six major river-systems where most industries and major towns were located. Rivers were dug deeper, locks provided, and 'cuts' – artificial river beds – straightened bends.

London received fresh foods such as fish by relays of horses. The horses, geese and turkeys from Norfolk, cattle from Scotland and Wales, packhorses in trains of up to forty, and covered wagons all churned up the roads.

The wealthy had coaches, but did not venture out in winter and bad weather. Parishes, with the use of six days of unpaid labour from villagers, were responsible for the upkeep of local roads, but main roads were very neglected.

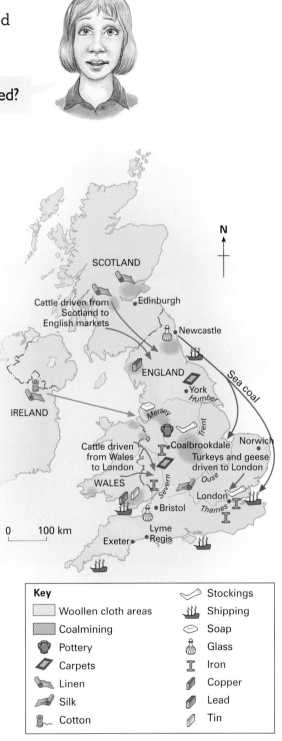

▲ Britain in 1750, showing the main occupations of the workers

In 1706 an Act adopted an earlier idea. Independent trustees were authorised to take over and rebuild sections of roads. Barriers with toll bars and pikes (spikes) were erected at each end, and users of the turnpikes paid a toll.

For every Horse, Mule, or other Cattle, drawing any Coach, or other Carriage, with springs the sum of _____ 4d

For every Horse, Mule or other Beast or Cattle drawing any Waggon, Cart or other such carriage, not employed solely in carrying or going empty to fetch Lime for manure the sum of _____ 3d

For every Horse, Mule, or other Beast or Cattle, drawing any Waggon, Cart, or other such Carriage employed solely in carrying or going empty to fetch Lime for manure the sum of _____ 1½d

For every Horse, Mule, or Ass, laden or unladen and not drawing, the sum of _____ 1d

For every Drove of Oxen, Cows, or other meat Cattle per score, the sum of _____ 10d

For every Drove of Calves, Sheep, Lambs or Pigs per score, the sum of _____ 5d

▲ Toll charges at Llanfair Gate in Wales

The Stuart dynasty	James I (James VI of Scotland)	Charles I	Charles II	James II	William III	and Mary II	Anne
	1603–1625	1625–1649	1649–1685	1685–1688	1688–1702	1688–1694	1702 March 18

THE LAST **2** STUART

Queen Anne

By the time Anne succeeded to the throne as Queen of England, Scotland and Ireland in 1702, she was in constant pain, rather stout, and suffering from gout. She had also endured seventeen pregnancies, including nine stillbirths, but all her children had died before her succession. She was the daughter of James II, but she did not reign until both her sister Mary died in 1694 and Mary's husband, William III, died in 1702.

▲ Anne, before she became Queen, with her longest-surviving child, William, who died aged 11

What happened to James Edward, the son of James II?

By his second marriage he became Catholic, like his father, so was barred from succeeding to the English throne.

After the Act of Succession of 1701, only Protestants who were specifically members of the Church of England could reign. The government was so determined to keep a Protestant on the throne that it even amended the Act so that the crown would, after Anne's death, go to a Protestant niece of James II, Princess Sophia, who through marriage had become Electress of Hanover, a German state.

The government was well aware that James II, in comfortable exile in France and protected by the Catholic King Louis XIV, had many supporters in England, the highlands of Scotland and in Ireland. These supporters were known as Jacobites, after the Latin 'Jacobus' for James.

In 1702 England went to war with France to drive Louis XIV's grandson, Philip V, from the throne of Spain and to prevent the dominance of France over Europe. Anne needed money from Scotland to help her fight the war. This put Scotland in a strong bargaining position.

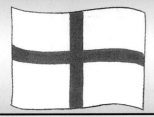

Cross of St George

Cross of St Andrew

Union Jack of 1707

A United Kingdom?

The Scots knew that the English needed their agreement for the Hanoverian succession. They also wanted a share in England's colonial trade. Since 1695, after an attempt to trade with Panama had been blocked by English merchants, Scotland had remained a poor country.

What did the Scots do?

In 1704 they passed an Act of Security.

This declared that the Scots would choose Anne's successor unless they were given equal trading rights. The Scottish Parliament would not grant Anne money for the war against France unless she signed. Anne did so.

The English Parliament retaliated with the Aliens Act of 1705. All Scots were to be treated as foreigners, and no Scottish goods were to be allowed into England unless the Scots recognised the Hanoverian succession in Scotland as well as England.

The two countries were on the brink of war, but the Scots did agree to discuss some form of union with England if the Aliens Act was withdrawn. So, not without misgivings on both sides, a Treaty of Union was negotiated and signed on May 1, 1707.

Terms of the Treaty of Union:

- The two kingdoms to be united into one and to be called Great Britain

- The United Kingdom to be represented by one Parliament of Great Britain

- Scots to agree to the Hanoverian succession

- All subjects to have freedom of trade and navigation

- The Scottish legal system to remain the same

- A common flag to be used

- The Kirk to remain the official Church of Scotland

- Customs, duties, coins, weights and measures to be standardised

- Scots to send 16 Lords and 45 MPs to Parliament

Anne's title was now Queen of Great Britain and Ireland.

▲ The Commissioners present the Treaty of Union to Queen Anne, 1707

The War of the Spanish Succession	Battle of Blenheim: British victory	Capture of Gibraltar	Battle of Ramillies: British victory	Battle of Oudenarde: British victory	Capture of Minorca	Battle of Malplaquet: British victory Heavy losses	Treaty of Utrecht: Received Newfoundland, Nova Scotia, Hudson Bay from French Kept Gibraltar and Minorca
1702–14	1704	1704	1706	1708	1708	1709	1714

The Duke of Marlborough

Extra finance from Scotland was needed, as fighting against France in the War of the Spanish Succession lasted until 1714. Anne made an experienced general, John Churchill, the Duke of Marlborough and Captain-General of the Allied armies. He was the husband of her court favourite, Sarah.

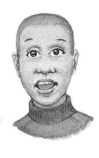

Who were the main allies?

Austria, the Netherlands and Portugal.

▲ The War of the Spanish Succession

Their aim was to recapture the Spanish Netherlands seized by Louis XIV and to drive his grandson Philip V off the throne of Spain. Fighting took place in the Netherlands, Central Europe and at sea.

Based at Lisbon, the Allies consolidated their position in the western Mediterranean by capturing Gibraltar (1704) and Minorca (1708).

On land, after driving the French from the Netherlands, Marlborough marched 400 miles into Bavaria to join Prince Eugene, the Austrian commander, to save Vienna from capture.

In 1704 at Blenheim he secured, after a hard-fought battle, a great victory and saved Austria. A grateful Parliament gave Marlborough the estate and medieval palace of Woodstock, later Blenheim Palace.

Marlborough next conquered Belgium by his victory at Ramillies in 1706. In 1708, with Eugene's support, he won the Battle of Oudenarde, and followed this with a five-month siege of Lille. In 1709 he was victorious at Malplaquet, but this led to allied casualties of over 16,000 against 11,000 French. The French commander Villars still barred the way to France.

The Churchills fell from favour before the end of the war but, helped by Marlborough's victories, the Treaty of Utrecht in 1714 gave Britain a new reputation in Europe and established her as a competitor to France.

▲ Marlborough at Blenheim

Death of Queen Anne	Elector of Hanover, George Guelph, succeeds as King of Great Britain and Ireland	Hanover's population $\frac{3}{4}$ million	Britain's population 5.9 million	Hanover and Britain ruled independently

1714

George I

THE FIRST **3** HANOVERIAN

When Anne died in 1714, Princess Sophia had already died, so Sophia's son George succeeded as King of Great Britain and Elector of Hanover at the age of 54.

Did he try to understand the British way of life?

George always expressed a preference for Hanover. Though he had known for some time he would very likely be king, he had not bothered to learn English. This language barrier and his shyness did present difficulties, both at court and in Parliament.

One aspect of the King's life was regarded with particular distaste all over Europe. His wife, Sophia, had become involved with a Swedish colonel, Count Koningsberg. This count mysteriously 'disappeared' and George divorced and then imprisoned Sophia, aged 28, in a castle for life. She died aged 59, without ever seeing her two children again.

▲ George I

Courtiers soon began to misunderstand and mock the king. His Turkish servants were regarded as odd, his German mistresses as ugly and his German and Huguenot ministers as foreign favourites.

Then, both mistresses were implicated in a gross fraud during a financial scandal. This involved the South Sea financial company which had received a contract from Parliament to take over £31 million of the National Debt.

Although its affairs were legalised, the company distributed shares at favourable prices to ministers, MPs and favourites. Shares rose and fortunes were made. The South Sea 'Bubble' burst because shares were over-valued. Panic selling followed and many people were financially ruined. Some MPs were suspected of accepting bribes and the political result was the fall of the government.

▲ The position of Hanover in Europe

House of Lords: 220 members, including 26 bishops, 16 Scottish peers	Members from same social background and agreed on important matters. Members of Commons often related to Members of Lords	House of Commons: 558 members, 24 representing Wales, 45 representing Scotland

1714

King, court and Parliament

The ministry and court were saved from the disaster of being implicated in the South Sea Bubble scandal by the parliamentary skills of a Whig minister, Robert Walpole.

Was the court important?

As the centre of the country's political and social life, it was very important.

▲ Robert Walpole, the first prime minister

Every decision and appointment had to be discussed with the King who controlled a vast system of patronage. It was his right as monarch to appoint ministers, bishops and Church livings, offer commissions in the armed forces, positions in the royal household and award peerages.

His chief ministers formed a small inner cabinet over which George I presided, but as he disliked his own son George, who interpreted for him and became rather bored, after 1718 he ceased to attend. A leading minister then presided over meetings. Robert Walpole assumed this role, which came to be referred to as 'prime minister', though at first this was not an official title.

During the reigns of William III and Anne, the Whigs and Tories had been two distinct parties. The Tories traditionally championed the interests of the landed gentry, the established Church and the Crown. The Whigs traditionally championed the interests of the merchants and lawyers, the Dissenters and Parliament.

In the reign of George I the situation changed. The Whigs persuaded the King that *they* were the true supporters of the Hanoverian dynasty.

How were they able to do that?

Some important Tories had decided to back a Jacobite rebellion led by James Edward, the son of James II, to place the Stuarts back on the throne.

▲ The House of Commons in the early eighteenth century

The 'Fifteen' and the 'Forty-five'

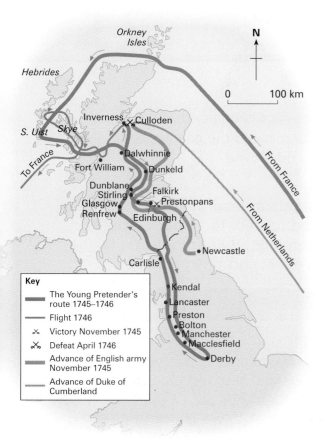

▲ The 'Forty-five'

Why did James Edward fail?

James had the support of Louis XIV, the Catholic Highland class, a few Tory peers and Jacobites in exile, but the rebellion of 1715 failed because of insufficient finance and poor leadership.

The government, well informed of Jacobite plans by spies, was never seriously threatened, and the rising petered out. The second rebellion of 1745, during the reign of George II, was much more threatening.

Charles Edward, son of James Edward, took advantage of the fact that most British troops were abroad at war with France. He landed with seven clansmen on the west coast of Scotland. Persuaded by his considerable personal charm, some clans rallied, and an early victory was secured at Prestonpans.

Charles hoped for a general rising, but when this was not forthcoming he marched towards London. English Jacobites failed to rally in support, so at Derby the Scots turned round and retreated to Inverness.

At Culloden Moor the 5,000 exhausted troops were cut down by 9,000 English troops under the Duke of Cumberland, son of George II. Cumberland ruthlessly pursued the defeated and killed the wounded, earning the nickname 'the Butcher'.

Charles escaped but 1,100 of his followers were transported or banished; over 80 were tried and executed; and laws were passed to destroy the legal hereditary power of clan chiefs. Clansmen had to give up their weapons and tartan kilts.

Culloden was the last battle fought on British soil and marked the end of Stuart claims to the throne of Great Britain.

▲ Culloden Moor, April 16 1745

New laws meant Catholics could not:						
Vote or become MPs	Go to university	Be lawyers, teachers or soldiers	Hold any government jobs	Buy land from a Protestant	Own horses worth over £5	Limited rights to inheritance and secure leases
1690						1703

Ireland

Was there a Union with Ireland at this time?

No, because unlike Scotland, Ireland was a conquered land with no bargaining powers. Protestants had dominated the country since the defeat of James II at the Battle of the Boyne.

Though only a quarter of the population, the Protestants formed the Irish Parliament, the Church of Ireland and the social elite, and owned most of the land. Centred around Dublin, they represented the Protestant Ascendancy. Other Protestants, the Scottish Presbyterian settlers, were centred round Belfast and prospered as merchants.

The Catholics, although forming about three-quarters of the population, had few rights and owned only 3 per cent of the land. This meant that many rented land from the Protestant landowners who were often absent in England. The farmers and investors who rented the land then sub-let it as 'middlemen' to the poorest, landless Catholics, the cottiers.

The cottiers, after handing over two-thirds of their produce in rent, had to pay a hearth tax and tithes to the Protestant clergy of the Church of Ireland. Desperately poor, they relied increasingly on the potato to feed their growing families. One acre of land planted with potatoes could feed a family of six, year after year.

▲ The Duke of Dorset's state ball, Dublin Castle, 1731. All the important Protestant families of Ireland were there

In the early eighteenth century some aspects of Irish life improved. Turnpike roads and inland waterways were improved. The cattle-breeding and butter-making industries flourished, as did the linen industry in the Protestant north.

English laws hampered some trade. In 1699 woollen cloth could be exported only to England where it was charged heavy duties. When a brewing industry was started, Ireland could only import hops from England and these, too, were charged duties.

Trade, wealth and power

THE BRITISH 4 EMPIRE

▲ The British Empire, 1713

Why was Ireland prevented from developing certain industries?

For the same reason that Scotland was prevented from trading with Panama. The British government wanted to protect her own manufacturers from any foreign competition.

Hanoverian politicians knew that it was trade that was the cause of Britain's increasing wealth, and that it was wealth that gave countries power. To protect her manufacturers and merchants, Britain, in common with other European colonial powers, adopted a method called the Mercantile System.

By a series of complex Navigation Acts they ensured that their manufacturers and merchants were protected from competition from other nations:

- All trade to and from the colonies had to be carried in British or colonial ships.

- The colonies had to purchase all their manufactured goods via Britain. This gave Britain a guaranteed market for her manufacturers.

- The colonies were not allowed to compete with Britain in the production of certain goods such as woollen cloth.

- Important crops from the plantations, such as sugar from the West Indies and tobacco from Virginia, could only be sent to countries in the British Empire. This meant Britain could re-export the surplus to the Continent for vast profits.

- In the 1720s and 1730s Robert Walpole removed customs duties on British exports and on imported raw materials. He kept high duties on imports from foreign manufacturers.

Britain was even prepared to go to war with other nations to protect and enlarge her colonies. Her main rival was her old enemy, France.

Robert Clive sails to India age 19	Idle misfit at home	Clerk for East India Company at Madras	Escapes from Madras disguised as Indian interpreter	Shows flair for command at siege of Arcot	Toast of London Made MP	Lieutenant-Colonel 2nd in command	War in Bengal
1744			1746	1751	1753	1755	1756

India

The Union Jack flew over three main trading factories in India – in Madras, Bombay and Calcutta – all owned by the East India Company.

The French flag flew over two factories of the French India Company, in Pondicherry and Chandernagore.

▲ Surat, an early trading factory

Were the factories warehouses?

No, they were actual communities – settlements fortified by European and Indian (sepoy) troops against bandit and local tribal warfare.

▲ Map of India in the early eighteenth century, showing exports

The governor of Pondicherry, Dupleix, had personal ambitions to rule over southern India. In 1746 he took the opportunity, while Britain and France were on opposing sides in the War of the Austrian Succession, to send a fleet to take over Madras. In return the British besieged Pondicherry, but failed to secure it.

Although Madras was restored when war ended, Dupleix moved once more against the British. He placed a 'puppet' nawab (governor) on the throne of the Carnatic in south India, and supported him with French and Sepoy troops. The East India Company sponsored a rival nawab and supported him with British and sepoy troops.

The British candidate was besieged by his French rival at Trichinopoly. To entice troops away from Trinchinopoly the British sent 200 soldiers, 300 sepoys and three field-guns to Arcot, the capital of the Carnatic. Under a young captain, Robert Clive, they took it against a force twice their size and held it for fifty days. When reinforcements arrived the French were defeated.

Clive, a former clerk for the Company was fêted as a hero in India and in England. He was made Lieutenant-Colonel, second in command of the Company's forces in the south. In 1756 he was called north to Bengal.

Black Hole of Calcutta	Battle of Plassey			Clive Governor of Bengal	Lord Clive: Two English homes One Irish estate London house MP for Shrewsbury	Clive commits suicide
	Clive 1,000 European troops, 2,000 sepoys, 8 cannon, 1 howitzer		Siraj 50,000 cavalry and infantry, bullock-drawn cannon, elephants			
1756 June 20	1757 June 23				1760	1774

Nawabs and nabobs

The Nawab of Bengal, Siraj-ud-Daula, had picked a quarrel with the East India Company and had marched on the Calcutta settlement. Most of the British fled, but about 65 were captured and held overnight in a small room. The night of June 20, 1756 was particularly oppressive as the monsoon was imminent. By morning about 43 people had died. The incident became known as the Black Hole of Calcutta.

In one sortie Clive recaptured Calcutta and went on to take the French settlement of Chandernagore. Defying all instructions, he then put up another candidate, Mir Jafar, to replace Siraj-ud-Daula. At the Battle of Plassey, Clive won an overwhelming victory against Siraj-ud-Daula, though he had only 3,000 troops against 50,000.

▲ The Battle of Plassey, 1757: Clive receives tribute from Mir Jafar

What effect did the battle have?

Over the next three years French influence in India was destroyed and the East India Company became a major military power within India.

Clive became governor of Bengal, a province so fertile that the Indians called it paradise on earth. It was soon providing 60 per cent of all Asian imports into Britain. Company officials, including Clive, received personal gifts from Mir Jafar, arranged trading conditions to suit themselves, pocketed surplus revenues and traded privately in salt, opium and diamonds.

On their return home many individuals were wealthy enough to buy huge estates in Ireland or England, setting themselves up as country gentlemen and buying seats in Parliament. Some envious English nicknamed these superior upstarts 'nabobs'.

By the 1770s the government was so alarmed at the greed and corruption of the Company, it began to take over control.

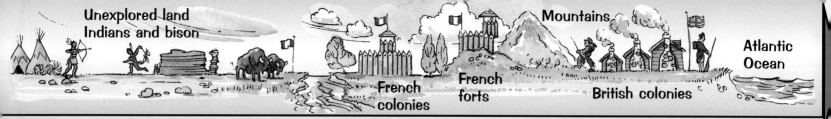

Canada

The French were also rivals of Britain in North America.

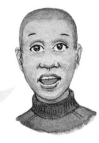

Did they have trading factories there?

No, like the British they were settlers, having founded Quebec in the north in 1608.

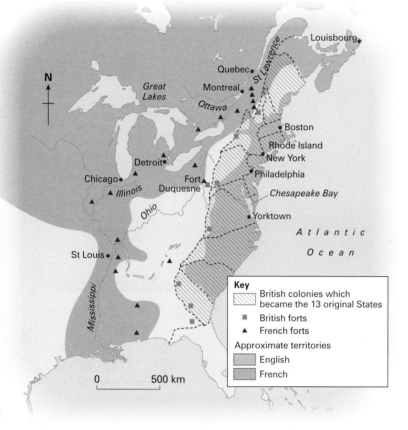

▲ North America in the 1750s

Key

//// British colonies which became the 13 original States

■ British forts

▲ French forts

Approximate territories

English

French

The French had gained territory by sailing south down the St Lawrence from Quebec and north up the Mississippi. They built forts especially where their territory was close to that of the British. They wanted to expand east to the rich lands near the coast, with the support of most Indian tribes who were hunters and trappers like themselves. The British wanted to expand west for more farming land. Clashes were inevitable.

In 1755 Britain sent troops under General Bradshaw to help the Virginian colonies expel the French from their new stronghold, Fort Duquesne. The British forces were defeated and tensions along the frontier increased.

When Britain entered the Seven Years' War against France in 1756, Pitt, the Prime Minister, decided on the complete conquest of the French in North America. After a long siege, the British took the major stronghold of Louisbourg in 1758.

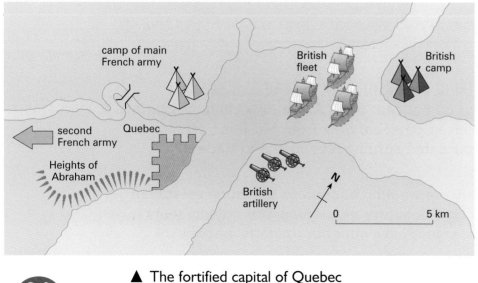

▲ The fortified capital of Quebec

The fleet, commanded by General Wolfe, could now sail up the St Lawrence River for an assault on Quebec. Wolfe's transport was protected by twenty-two warships whose skilled navigators, including an officer called James Cook, charted a course through little-known waters. Quebec stood high above the river, defended by a hundred guns and an army under Montcalm, a brilliant French commander. Montcalm was confident that he could defeat the British by guerrilla warfare and by waiting for winter to drive them away.

Assault on Quebec

What did Wolfe do?

He ordered his troops to scale the cliffs to reach the plain called the Heights of Abraham. He thought that if he could capture this, the French would be forced to fight.

At 2 am on the night of September 12 1759, British warships bombarded the town to draw attention away from the attack. Shielded by darkness and using the expected arrival of a French convoy carrying provisions as cover, 1,700 troops were ferried to a cove at the base of the cliffs. An advance party of twenty-eight soldiers reached the top and overpowered the sentries. Within two hours 3,000 troops followed, a few of them hauling cannon. At daybreak the astonished French faced an enemy drawn up in battle lines.

Montcalm sent orders for his second army to prepare to attack from behind, but prepared his own 10,000 men for immediate battle. At 10 am his soldiers advanced, arranged in three tightly packed formations, firing occasional shots. Though shot in the wrist and groin, Wolfe continued to walk along the front line telling his men to hold fire. Only when the French were as close as thirty metres did he give the order to fire.

▲ The battle for Quebec

▲ The death of Wolfe

The first line volley was followed by an equally devastating round from the second line. The French wavered, broke rank and fled. Wolfe ordered a bayonet charge. At this moment he was shot again; he died hearing of victory. Montcalm, equally courageous, was also killed.

The French retreated to Montreal. When this was taken a year later, the British gained control over North America.

The Pacific Ocean

It was the outstanding mapping and leadership skills shown by James Cook during the assault on Quebec that led the Admiralty to appoint him to take part in a joint scientific and secret mission in the Pacific Ocean.

The scientists were to observe the passage of the planet Venus and to collect and catalogue creatures and plants. There was always the possibility that new 'cash crops' such as tobacco or sugar might be unearthed.

What was the secret mission?

Britain wanted to remain the dominant maritime nation of the world and needed accurate maps of the Pacific, its islands and their anchorages. There was some urgency as a French navigator had been observed sailing in the area.

This voyage was also a chance to search for a mysterious continent that lay somewhere south of America and Africa. During the voyage (1769–1771) Cook mapped and, with the backing of British law, annexed (took possession of) New Zealand, Australia and many Pacific islands for the British Crown.

Did the native peoples want this?

Their wishes were ignored. The Aborigines of Australia, for example, were regarded as nomads who did not till the ground, and seemed to lack any social organisation or religion.

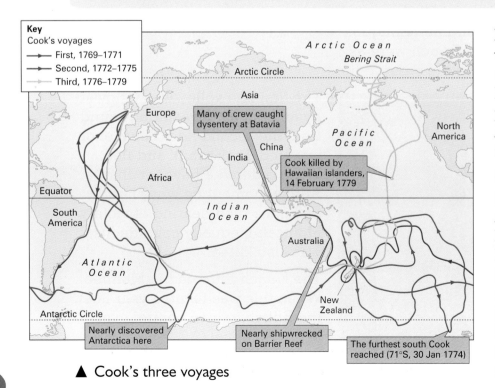

▲ Cook's three voyages

During a second historic voyage (1772–1775) Cook sailed further south and for longer than any person previously. He reached the Antarctic Circle, just failing to find Antarctica.

Cook's third voyage (1776–1779) ended tragically. After helping to discover the North-West passage around North America, he was hacked to death by hostile natives in Hawaii during a brawl over the theft of a small boat. The Hawaiians did, however, give this remarkable man a hero's funeral.

Union of Indian tribes attacks forts	Sugar Act	Stamp Act	Stamp Act repealed	Peace signed with Indians	Government forces of 10,000 kept in America
1763	1764	1765		1766	

THE AMERICAN WAR OF INDEPENDENCE

5

America

By the 1770s, after gaining Canada from the French and new territories in the Pacific Ocean, Britain had become the world's leading colonial and maritime power. Through discoveries, settlements, trading factories and war, she had added to her first colony of Virginia, founded in 1620.

After gaining Canada, thousands of English, Scots and Irish emigrated to join the two and a half million settlers already in North America. They began to move into the mid-west and onto land taken from the Indians.

In 1763 the Indian tribes, having lost the support of the French and fearing for their hunting grounds, attacked frontier posts. Peace was signed in 1766, but the British government felt that the colonists should pay for the cost of maintaining British forces in America.

▲ The thriving port of Boston

To raise revenue, Britain imposed customs duties on certain goods, but it was an internal tax, the Stamp Act of 1765, which caused an outcry. This Act charged a fee on every commercial and legal document – wills, licences, certificates, even newspapers and playing cards. There were demonstrations in most colonies, burning of stamps and boycotting of imported goods.

Why such a response?

The Americans resented the fact that a government 3,000 miles away should make such decisions.

These third-generation colonists were very different from the original pilgrims of the *Mayflower*. They had built up businesses, banks, warehouses and ports, established professions and opened universities. They decided to make a stand over their constitutional rights.

They argued that since they did not elect MPs to attend Parliament at Westminster, Parliament should not impose taxes on them. As loyal and freeborn Englishmen, they wanted to be represented. 'No taxation without representation' was their cry.

The Boston Massacre and Tea Party

What did Britain do?

It withdrew the Stamp Act, but the Americans continued to resist new taxes on tea and manufactured goods – and there were further disturbances.

▲ The Boston Massacre, 1770

The British stationed a garrison at Boston, Massachusetts, a particular trouble spot. In 1770 a scuffle broke out between Boston youths who taunted some soldiers. Blows turned into a riot, the army opened fire and civilians were killed. The incident became known as the Boston Massacre.

In 1772 another incident increased tension. A British customs ship, the *Gaspée*, ran aground off Rhode Island while chasing a ship suspected of smuggling. A group of islanders boarded the *Gaspée*, burnt it and wounded the captain.

The British government decided to withdraw all duties except one. As a mark of its continuing authority, it kept the duty on tea. This led to another incident.

▲ The Boston Tea Party, 1773

Under a Tea Act of 1773, the East India Company, which had a surplus of tea, was allowed to ship cargo direct from India to America and set up her own agencies in the colonies. This monopoly of trade angered not only American merchants who still had to pay tax, but smugglers, because the Company's tea was cheaper than theirs!

In 1773 the British ship *Dartmouth*, with a cargo of East India Company tea, sailed into Boston harbour. A group of local rebels called Sons of Liberty, disguised as Mohawk Indians, clambered on board that and two other ships. They broke open tea-chests with tomahawks and hurled the contents into the sea. Other 'tea parties', including one in New York, also took place.

Growing conflict

How did Britain respond?

With firm action.

By a series of Intolerable Acts, Britain increased the power of the Governor of Massachusetts, based in Boston. He could now send Bostonians for trial in Britain, close the port of Boston and ban public meetings. Such powers given to a Governor angered the Americans.

The American system of government was, in fact, very democratic. Men and women (not slaves) had equal voting rights and held elections to choose legislative assemblies (state parliaments). Yet any decisions made by the assemblies could be set aside by the British-appointed governors whose own decisions could be imposed without discussion.

In 1774 Americans were angered further by the Quebec Act which separated Canada from America. Canada's land was extended to the north of the River Ohio and east of the Mississippi, thus ending fifty years of expansion by the settlers. At a meeting of Congress (Parliament) at Philadelphia, delegates from the colonies, while declaring their loyalty to the Crown, demanded the repeal of all acts passed since 1767.

What would this mean?

The end of Britain's control over the colonies, something which many rebels wanted.

What finally led to open rebellion was a confrontation at Lexington, Massachusetts. The port of Boston had been closed by Governor-General Gage. In April 1775 Gage sent troops to destroy an illegal ammunition store set up by rebels at Concord, near Boston. En route, Gage's troops scattered attacking rebels at Lexington, then went on to destroy the store. On their return, they were again attacked by the rebels. 273 British soldiers – but only 100 rebels – were killed. This was the spark for war.

▲ American rebels

Bunker's Hill: British victory	Rebels fail to take Canada	British withdraw from Boston	Declaration of Independence	British successes around New York	Princetown and Trenton: British defeats	Brandywine Creek: British victory	Saratoga: British defeat
1775 June	1776	1776	1776 July 4	1776–1777			1777

The American War of Independence

Was this a civil war?

Many British and Americans thought so, as they had always regarded themselves as belonging to one country. The prospect of war filled them with disbelief and dismay, and many colonists remained loyal to the British Crown.

The war began well for the British when they drove the Massachusetts army from Bunker's Hill, overlooking Boston, and defeated rebels attacking Montreal and Quebec. In 1776, however, the United Colonial Army under George Washington forced the British to withdraw from Boston.

This success encouraged some rebels to push for a Declaration of Independence during a Congress meeting in July 1776. The main writer of this momentous document was Thomas Jefferson. It included this famous passage:

> *We hold these truths to be self-evident, that all men are created equal, that they are endowed by their creator with certain unalienable* rights; that among these are life, liberty, and the pursuit of happiness.*

*rights that cannot be surrendered

▲ Signing the Declaration of Independence, July 4 1776

It was accepted and signed by members of Congress, and marked the severance of all links with Britain.

Britain had expected an early victory, but against sharpshooting Americans engaged in guerrilla warfare this proved difficult. In 1777 the British general Howe captured New York. He was expected to meet up with General Burgoyne who had left Canada with 8,000 troops. Their combined forces would isolate the New England colonies and lead to a swift end to the war.

But Howe did not wait for Burgoyne. After defeating Washington at Brandywine Creek he marched on to capture Philadelphia. Burgoyne reached Saratoga but, outnumbered by rebels, surrendered. Howe failed to keep Philadelphia.

In 1778 the war became a global struggle.

France and Spain enter war to support America	Savannah captured by British	Charleston captured by British	Defeat of British troops at Yorktown	Treaty of Versailles recognises USA	Washington is world's first President
1778–1779	1778 December	1780 May	1781 October 17	1783	1789

The United States of America

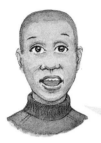

Why did the war become a global one?

In February 1778 France entered the war in support of the American rebels.

Suddenly Britain needed protection for troop convoys; naval forces were needed to defend the shores of Britain; the West Indies had to be defended; and reinforcements had to be sent to India to defend British interests there.

Then, in June 1779, Spain entered the war in support of America. Britain required further reinforcements and armed supply-convoys for Minorca and Gibraltar, and West Florida came under attack. Britain's naval power was stretched to breaking point.

In 1779 Britain enlisted black slaves into their forces by offering freedom to any slave belonging to a rebel. Thousands joined, many working as labourers or looking after transport trains.

In 1780, under General Cornwallis, Britain captured Charleston and won control of South Carolina and Georgia. In 1781 Cornwallis attempted to control North Carolina and Virginia. Meanwhile, the French fleet, by moving into Chesapeake Bay, stopped supplies reaching the British camp at Yorktown.

▲ General Cornwallis, surrounded by French and American troops, surrenders to Washington. The French general, the Marquis de La Fayette, and his men took back to France some of the American ideas of liberty and equality

Washington made the 50-mile dash from New York to Yorktown. Cornwallis, outnumbered, isolated and under bombardment, surrendered on October 17 1781. The defeat marked the end of the war.

The Treaty of Versailles in 1783 recognised the independence of the United States of America. In 1789 George Washington became America's first President. The loss of the American colonies was a huge blow to the prestige and pride of Britain.

George III

The Hanoverian monarch on the throne during the American War of Independence was George III, who began his reign in 1760, aged 22.

Was he involved in discussions about the war or, like George I, was he uninterested in Britain?

George III was very involved in the affairs of his country and felt the loss of the colonies deeply. He tended to blame his ministers rather than himself when wrong decisions were made, but he did become reconciled to the loss.

George III's first public announcement as King was 'Born and educated in this country, I glory in the name of Britain.' George spoke English without a German accent, which pleased his subjects.

Sadly, he was afflicted with a terrible malady which led to bouts of insanity, and blindness and deafness in old age. But before it destroyed his mind, he showed genuine interest in what was going on in his country. He acquainted himself with artists and merchants and the new manufacturers. These included people such as the potter Josiah Wedgwood, who was establishing himself as a manufacturer of porcelain on a large scale.

▲ George III and Queen Charlotte with six of their fifteen children, 1770

The King was widely read, particularly about agriculture, and wrote letters to an agricultural journal under a pseudonym. At Windsor he had three farms of over 1,000 acres in all. He imported and bred the ancestors of merino sheep. His interest in farming led to an affectionate nickname: 'Farmer George'.

◀ A picture of the time, depicting George III as a patron of the arts (Britain is represented by the figure of Britannia)

Sow four grains in a row,
One for the pigeon, one for the crow,
One to rot and one to grow

| Broadcast sowing | Birds a menace | Uneven growth | Laborious hand-weeding |

Jethro Tull

Other wealthy landowners, as well as the king, were interested in agricultural improvements. One early improver was Jethro Tull, who observed that many farming methods were wasteful, particularly broadcasting (sowing of seed) by hand. To make sowing more efficient, he invented a seed-drill. This horse-drawn machine in one operation scratched a channel at a regular depth in the soil, dropped the grain at regular intervals, then covered it with soil.

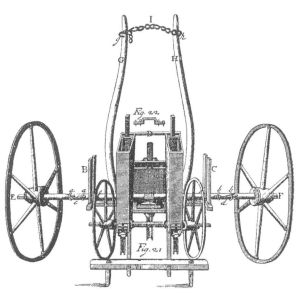

▲ Jethro Tull's seed-drill

Tull was wealthy enough to travel abroad. On his travels he noticed that French farm workers hoed between the rows of grapes. This let air into the roots of plants and cleared out weeds. Crop yields were heavier as the weeds did not rob the vines of sunlight and water.

On his return to his Berkshire estates, Tull divided the land into long narrow plots. Women workers weeded the spaces between the rows of crops, using hand-held hoes. Tull's next step was to fix the hoe onto a framework on wheels, with the blade set just below the surface. This device was harnessed to horses which moved between the rows, uprooting weeds.

In 1733 Tull described some of his work with horse-drawn iron implements such as harrows and rakes in his book, *The New Horse Hoeing Husbandry* (farming).

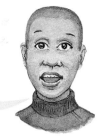

So did he revolutionise agriculture?

In fact, some of his innovations were laughed at. Some ideas, such as not using manure as fertiliser, were faulty; but many farmers were reluctant to change old traditions and customs.

Other more progressive farmers, such as 'Turnip' Townshend, incorporated his ideas into their farm improvement schemes.

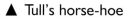 ▲ Tull's horse-hoe

	1730	1731	1732	1733	1734
Field A	Wheat	Turnips	Barley	Clover	Wheat
Field B	Turnips	Barley	Clover	Wheat	Turnips
Field C	Barley	Clover	Wheat	Turnips	Barley
Field D	Clover	Wheat	Turnips	Barley	Clover
'Norfolk' rotation					

'Turnip' Townshend

'Turnip' was a nickname given to Viscount Charles Townshend who, during his time as a diplomat in Holland, had also observed the four-course rotation of crops used there. On his return home to his estate in Norfolk, he decided to adopt this method.

FIELD B

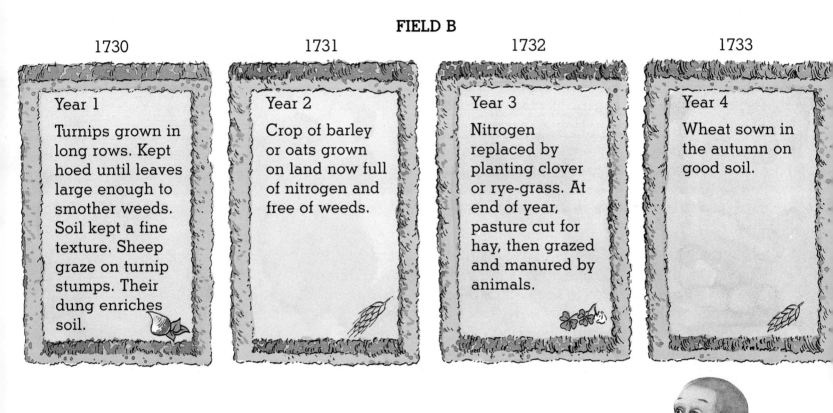

1730

Year 1

Turnips grown in long rows. Kept hoed until leaves large enough to smother weeds. Soil kept a fine texture. Sheep graze on turnip stumps. Their dung enriches soil.

1731

Year 2

Crop of barley or oats grown on land now full of nitrogen and free of weeds.

1732

Year 3

Nitrogen replaced by planting clover or rye-grass. At end of year, pasture cut for hay, then grazed and manured by animals.

1733

Year 4

Wheat sown in the autumn on good soil.

I can see the advantages. No field was left unused and fallow for a year as in the three-course rotation of crops.

It also meant that animals no longer had to be killed off in the autumn because of lack of fodder. Turnips and hay provided winter fodder. Fresh meat and milk in winter helped people to remain healthier.

Townshend also encouraged his tenant farmers to improve the condition of their soil by mixing the poorer sandy topsoil with the marl, a chalky, mineral-rich clay which lay underneath. The soil was then able to hold more moisture and nutrients. He used Tull's seed-drill and horse-hoe, and advocated the digging of drainage ditches in heavy, marshy land to prevent crops becoming waterlogged and disease-ridden.

Townshend gave his tenants long leases to give them time to make improvements. He also built a turnpike road to help farmers transport produce more quickly to nearby towns.

Average weight of livestock at Smithfield Market, London			Black cattle			
		166 kg	Black cattle	360 kg		
		8 kg	Lambs	22 kg		
		22 kg	Calves	66 kg		
		13 kg	Sheep	36 kg		
Before	1700			1800	After	

Out-breeding and in-breeding

Turnpike roads helped another Norfolk landowner, Thomas Coke, who, from 1776, owned land at Holkham near Townshend's estates. He carried on improvements already put in place by his family – the marling, the four-crop rotation, the underground drainage. He introduced special grasses for better hay, and employed Tull's seed-drill and the Rotherham plough, which used horses rather than oxen for ploughing.

In 1778 he decided to hold an agricultural festival at Holkham. As well as demonstrations of sheep-shearing, there were ploughing competitions, displays of farm machinery and viewings of his livestock.

Up to 7,000 people travelled along country roads to attend, admire and learn. People came from all over Britain and Europe to see the work of another improver, the selective breeder Robert Bakewell of Leicestershire.

▲ Sheep-shearing at Woburn, 1811

How did he select animals for breeding?

Firstly, he followed the usual method, that is 'cross-' or 'out-breeding', and mated animals of different breeds, hoping that their young would combine the best from both sides.

▲ The New Leicester

He took the Old Leicester (used for mutton) and the Lincoln (used for wool). After crossing, he then 'in-bred' them, that is mated sheep from the same family. The new Leicestershire improved breed had a long fleece and produced a lot of fatty mutton.

He experimented with other animals, and though none of his breeds survived, his approach to selective breeding, such as keeping pedigrees, does.

These wealthy improvers owned land of up to 2,000 acres. It made common sense for them to enclose their land rather than leave it under the old open-field system.

Squire:	Parson (rector):	Farmers:	Labourers:	Squatters:
Owned most land Lived in manor house Acted as Justice of the Peace	Owned land (glebe) Received a tithe	Freeholders owned land Smallholders rented land from squire or freeholders	'Lived in' on farm or in cottages with gardens	Built shacks on commons or wasteland: no legal rights

The farming community

Open and enclosed

What were enclosed fields?

These were the old open fields – with their strips of land, the commons and wasteland – converted into separate farms by hedges, ditches and fences.

Sheep farmers had been enclosing fields since the sixteenth century, as it made sense to keep the different breeds apart to control breeding and reduce the spread of disease. Enclosing the sheep prevented them from wandering over hectares of common land and losing flesh from their bones.

By the 1740s there were more enclosures as farms realised the benefits, particularly the financial ones.

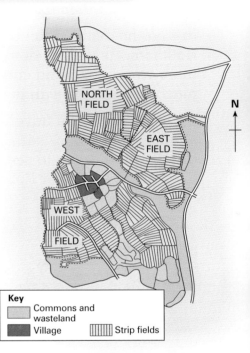

▲ Pre-enclosure map, Aston Blank, Gloucestershire, 1752

Once the commons and wasteland were enclosed, for example, land could be ploughed and put under a four-course rotation of crops. The farmer could produce a greater quantity and variety of food such as potatoes, turnips and swedes. More fodder for the animals all the year round meant more milk, more dairy produce and fresh meat. Family diets began to improve.

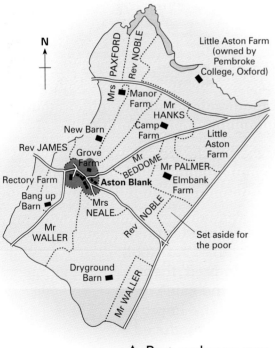

▲ Post-enclosure map of Aston Blank, 1882

The farmer could also make his own decisions about what to grow and how to improve his land. Instead of farming strips a long way apart and sowing the same crop at the same time as everybody else, he could experiment and had plenty of room to turn round one of the new machines.

How was it decided who could have which pieces of land?

Up to about 1740 enclosures took place as a result of general agreement amongst the villagers. It was easier to decide on new boundaries if there was one landowner. After 1740 enclosures usually required an Act of Parliament.

Number of Parliamentary Enclosure Acts	156	425	642	287	506	906	Nearly 3 million hectares enclosed in 18th century
	1751–1760	1761–1770	1771–1780	1781–1790	1791–1800	1801–1810	

How enclosures worked

In 1795 the parish of Aston Blank, for example, had five main landowners including the Lord of the Manor, the Reverend Mungo H. Noble, and the vicar, the Reverend Frederick James. They owned 80 per cent of the parish land and wanted to enclose the fields. They therefore followed certain procedures.

After meeting first, they fixed a notice to the church door to inform villagers that they would petition Parliament for an Act of Enclosure. Any objectors had three weeks to make their complaints known to the landowners.

Parliament would ask MPs, usually from the same county as the petitioners, to form a committee to examine the plans, hear complaints and make changes. Plans were usually approved and Parliament would pass an Act ordering the village to be enclosed.

Under the Act, a group of commissioners, three in the case of Aston Blank (all country gentlemen), visited the parish to divide, set out and allot the land. Once they had valued the land to be divided, they investigated claims, settled disputes and produced a map. Surveyors measured up the strips, re-drew the map with the new fields, roads, footpaths, drains and tracks all marked. The commissioners signed the map, which was stored in the church.

▲ Surveyors measuring out village land in about 1790

Who paid for all the enclosure work?

The landowners of the enclosed land.

Aston Blank's seven new owners had to pay expenses to cover the cost of obtaining the Act, and the solicitors', commissioners' and surveyors' fees. They also had to pay for the cost of fencing the allotments, making the public roads, for hedges and for clover seed to be sown in the allotments. Enclosure was expensive. Smaller farmers sometimes had to sell their land to the highest bidder when they found that they could not meet the costs.

Landscape gardener: Capability Brown	Furniture designers: Thomas Chippendale Thomas Sheraton	Architects: James Gibb William Kent Adam brothers	Portrait and landscape painters: Joshua Reynolds Thomas Gainsborough	Negro servants and boys became fashionable	Herds of wild deer decreased	Fox and hare hunted with packs of hounds

Wealth and leisure

Results of the enclosures

▲ Knight's Hill, Surrey, in about 1780

This picture captures beautifully the changes that occurred in the English countryside in the eighteenth and nineteenth centuries. In the foreground you can see a traditional working open-field. Behind this is an enclosed field with its boundary of fencing and hedges.

In the background is the palatial home with its own park. The owner could plant trees for game cover, for timber, to enhance the beauty of his estate and to display his wealth. Enclosures produced a pleasing landscape, rather like a patchwork quilt over the rich bed of English earth.

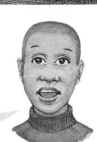

Who lived in these mansions?

The landed gentry – the gentleman farmers, squires and their families and nabobs.

The interiors were magnificent – with libraries, porcelain from Europe, furniture by Chippendale, paintings by Renaissance old masters, wallpaper from China and statues from Italy. Much was brought back by the young men of the family during their Grand Tour of the continent undertaken between university and Parliament. Hunting and shooting were favourite pastimes, and the jumping quality of horses became important.

By 1790 there were about 400 aristocratic families and 1,200 to 1,300 landed gentry who owned half of England's land. Owning land was still the base for prestige and wealth.

▲ Robert Gwillym of Atherton, Warwickshire, 1750

Poverty and poaching

▲ Inside a poor labourer's cottage

For the landless agricultural labourer and the smallholding cottagers, enclosures meant the loss of traditional rights – the right to graze their cows, and the right to gather turf and wood for fuel from the common and wasteland.

Before the enclosures women and children who gleaned the corn after the harvest could store enough to make bread for up to six months. After the enclosures, as they had no claim in law on their cottages, the number and poverty of those who owned no property grew.

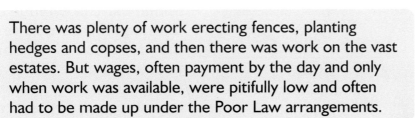

Enclosures must have provided work.

There was plenty of work erecting fences, planting hedges and copses, and then there was work on the vast estates. But wages, often payment by the day and only when work was available, were pitifully low and often had to be made up under the Poor Law arrangements.

After about 1710, as the population rapidly increased, the burden on the parish and farmers who paid the poor rate (the tax for poor relief) grew. The poor felt they had a traditional right to poach: often it meant the choice between starvation and survival.

Parliament – made up of landowners – disagreed. The Game Laws restricted the killing of birds and animals and protected the interests of the sportsmen with leisure to hunt. After 1770 the Game Laws became more severe and poachers retaliated by hunting in packs.

Heavy fines, imprisonment and transportation for trivial offences, such as the theft of a pheasant, followed. In 1803 resisting arrest for poaching became a capital offence (it carried the death penalty).

▲ Caught in the act of poaching

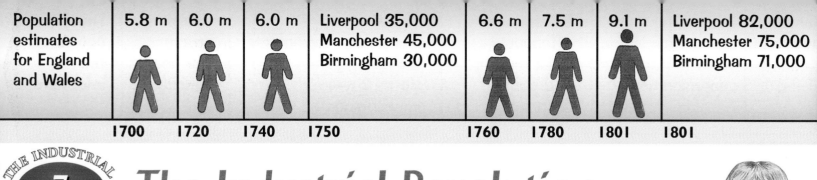

Population estimates for England and Wales	5.8 m	6.0 m	6.0 m	Liverpool 35,000 Manchester 45,000 Birmingham 30,000	6.6 m	7.5 m	9.1 m	Liverpool 82,000 Manchester 75,000 Birmingham 71,000
	1700	1720	1740	1750	1760	1780	1801	1801

The Industrial Revolution

Did the population increase because of improved farming methods and a better diet?

Gradually these did have an impact, and they also gave people a higher resistance to infection.

Many children still died of measles, chickenpox and diphtheria, though there were signs by 1760 that the battle against smallpox was slowly being won. Statistics show that epidemics of disease occurred in only 14 months between 1744 and 1784, yet there had been epidemics in 24 months between 1727 and 1730.

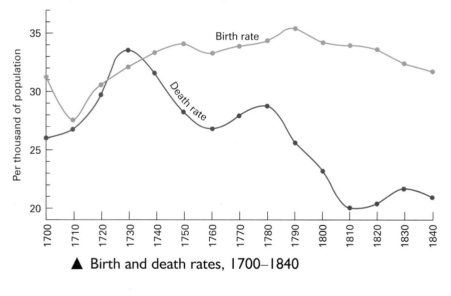

▲ Birth and death rates, 1700–1840

All these factors have a bearing on population figures, but what historians have also charted is the lowering of the age of marriage, particularly in areas such as South Lancashire, the West Riding of Yorkshire and the West Midlands. The average age of marriage fell from 27 to 24 and the proportion of unmarried people fell from 15 to 7 per cent. More earlier marriages meant more births and so more girls who would later produce families of their own.

Population grew in certain areas because from about 1760 there was a revolutionary change in the way many people worked. Industry moved from cottages into factories, and from villages into towns. The agricultural labourers moved to these towns to find work, and stayed there.

Uprooted from centuries of farming traditions, they formed a completely new society, surrounded by many more people. Life was not dominated by the landowner, the church, the seasons and the country calendar. It became dominated by businessmen, the factory, the discipline of regular and repetitive work, and machines.

The revolution began in the cottages and workshops of the spinners and weavers, with a simple invention.

Woollen industry stopped imports of Indian cotton goods	Home cotton industry grew	Wool – greasy, difficult for machines	Lambs took time to mature: cotton quick to grow	Imports of raw cotton increased	Cotton cheaper than wool

Cotton rather than wool

Revolution in the cotton industry

For centuries hand-loom weaving had been carried out in the same way. The shuttle, holding the weft yarn, was passed from one hand to another across the loom. The width of the cloth was limited by the length of the weaver's arms. If he had an assistant to catch and return the shuttle, he could make broader cloth (broadcloth).

In 1733 John Kay, a Lancashire weaver, invented the 'flying shuttle'. He put shuttle boxes at either side of the loom. The weaver pulled a lever, and hammers attached to the lever by cords struck the shuttle which 'flew' from one box to the other. The weaver could make wider cloth, no longer needed an assistant and could work faster.

▲ A simple, traditional hand loom

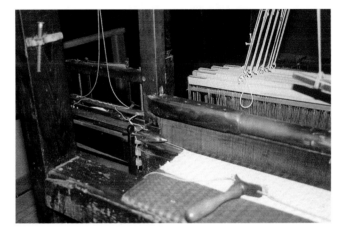

▲ The flying shuttle, 1733

Did Kay make money by selling his invention?

He patented it – that is, registered it with the government – and charged royalties for its use. But weavers and manufacturers refused to pay his charges. In 1753 fellow weavers, fearing his invention would put them out of work, wrecked his house. Kay fled and died in poverty in France. Yet his invention succeeded because of its simplicity.

▲ Kay, wrapped in a blanket, escapes from his home

The shuttle's success, however, presented a problem. Even before its invention it had taken about five or six spinners to keep a weaver supplied with yarn. Now far more yarn was needed.

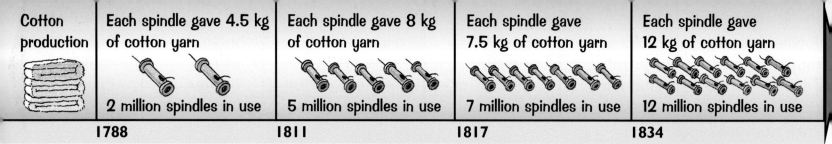

Cotton production	Each spindle gave 4.5 kg of cotton yarn	Each spindle gave 8 kg of cotton yarn	Each spindle gave 7.5 kg of cotton yarn	Each spindle gave 12 kg of cotton yarn
	2 million spindles in use	5 million spindles in use	7 million spindles in use	12 million spindles in use
	1788	1811	1817	1834

Spinning a yarn

Did people try to invent faster ways of spinning?

There were several attempts. One, patented in 1738 by Lewis Paul, was a roller-spinning device which drew out threads to required thicknesses before winding onto spindles. Five of Paul's machines were installed in the first cotton mill ever built, but they proved unreliable and the venture failed.

In 1761 the Society of Arts offered prizes for the invention of a machine that could 'spin six threads of wool, flax, hemp or cotton at a time and that will require but one person to work and attend it'. It was James Hargreaves who, in 1764, reproduced mechanically the action of a hand-spinner. His first 'spinning jenny' of eight spindles meant that the cottage spinner could rapidly increase the supply of yarn for the weaver.

Hargreaves too had his machinery destroyed, and moved from Blackburn to Nottingham where he became fairly prosperous. It was the next inventor of a spinning machine who was to make his fortune.

▲ From 8 to 16 spindles: a spinning jenny of about 1770

▲ Arkwright's water frame

In 1769 Richard Arkwright, by adapting the roller-spinning principles of Paul's machine, produced his water frame. Although this only spun four threads at a time, these threads were tougher than jenny-spun threads.

Once his idea was patented, Arkwright insisted that only larger models were made. These models needed water or horse power to work them, however, and could no longer fit into the spinners' homes.

What Arkwright had realised was the money-spinning potential of housing machines in factories, not cottages.

Birth of Richard Arkwright, youngest of 13	'Clean shave for a penny'	First patent for spinning machine	Partnership with Strutt	Water-powered mill, Cromford	Further patents for carding machines	Birkacre factory smashed	High Sheriff of Derbyshire	Knighted	Died at Willersley Castle
1732	1769		1771	1775	1779	1785	1786		1792

From wigs to wealth

Arkwright, a former barber and wigmaker, took huge financial risks in setting up his first factory in Cromford, near the River Derwent in Derbyshire.

Were factories a new invention too?

There had been a few silk mills run by the Combe brothers about 1717, from which Arkwright copied his factory ideas.

To do this he needed financial back-up (capital). He went into partnership with a capitalist, a wealthy stocking manufacturer, Jedidiah Strutt, who provided the capital. The first mill employed 200 to 300 workers. A second gave work to 800 more. In protest, in 1779 8,000 hand workers smashed up his mill near Birkacre in Lancashire.

Undaunted, Arkwright went on to own ten factories and sold his patent rights to other manufacturers, making his fortune in the process. He worked continuously from 5am to 9pm, travelling between his factories on relays of horses and improving and developing his machines.

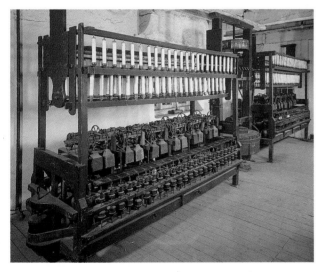

▲ From 4 spindles to 96: a water frame from the Cromford mill

Arkwright was a brilliant entrepreneur, taking over a business enterprise and making a profit from it. What was revolutionary about factory work was not just that the workers (labour) produced, in quantity, cheap cotton for millions of people (mass market), but that they produced the work under strict discipline and regimented working conditions.

When Arkwright was knighted in 1786, he felt his education had not fitted him for his social status. He was prepared, even when over fifty, to spend time each day improving his reading, writing and spelling. He died, immensely wealthy, at his unfinished home, Willersley Castle.

▲ The Cromford mill

1 skilled hand-loom weaver could weave 2 pieces of cloth per week, each 20 metres long	2,400 power looms in use	14,150 power looms in use	55,000 power looms in use	100,000 power looms in use	1 power-loom weaver attending 4 looms could weave 18–20 pieces of cloth per week, each 20 metres long
1800	1813	1820	1829	1833	1833

Crompton and Cartwright

Both Arkwright's water frame and Hargreave's jenny had drawbacks. The jenny spun fine yarn which snapped easily. The water frame spun coarser, tougher yarn which could only make cheaper quality cloth.

In 1779 a Bolton spinner, Samuel Crompton, invented a 'mule' which spun fine, good quality yarn that did not break.

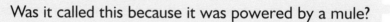

> Was it called this because it was powered by a mule?

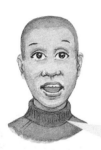

> No. Just as a mule is a cross between a horse and a donkey, this mule was a cross between the jenny and the water frame. Crompton took the best features of each to create a successful hybrid.

He designed it to be used in cottages, but it adapted perfectly to water and, later, steam power. Soon mules of 400 spindles were in operation. By the 1790s capitalists had seized on his invention and built more factories. Crompton could not afford to patent his mule, and by the time he was awarded £5,000 by Parliament in recognition of his achievement, others had made fortunes from his idea.

The invention of the American cotton gin in 1793 increased the supply of raw cotton so the hand-loom weavers now had a surplus of yarn and enjoyed high wages.

It was thought that a machine would never be able to replace the hand-loom weaver, or copy the complicated patterns of hand-woven linen damask and fancy woollens. In the 1780s, however, a clergyman, Edmund Cartwright, did produce a powered loom. Though his first machines were unwieldy, they succeeded in weaving plain cloth.

The hand-loom weavers fought back. In 1791 they burnt down Cartwright's factory in Manchester. But they were to fight a losing battle against the relentless march of machinery.

▲ Crompton's mule

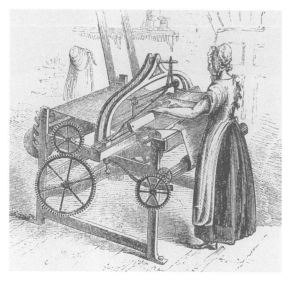

▲ Cartwright's power loom, about 1810

40

Piecers and scavengers

Who worked in the mills?

Crompton's mule required one adult to work it and several children to 'piece' together broken thread, 'scavenge' for fluff underneath the machines, remove full spindles and so forth. Early power looms required one adult and three or four children.

Mill owners paid adult workers, who either brought in their own children or paid for others' children. Some mill owners obtained children from paupers, or orphans from the Poor Law workhouses. Indeed, authorities were often pleased to be free of the responsibility of caring for them.

These children were housed, clothed and fed, and often worked unpaid, although they signed on as apprentices. As children had worked long hours before the Industrial Revolution, few questioned the age at which they began work (sometimes five) or the hours worked (often thirteen, even longer), or the conditions under which they worked (often temperatures of 21–25° C).

Some people, including a factory owner, Robert Owen, and Sir Robert Peel senior, did ask questions. Owen built not only mills but houses, shops, even schools for his employees. He refused to employ children under ten and cut working hours to ten and a half, still making a profit.

Owen, Peel and others campaigned for the Health and Morals of Apprentices Act, 1802. This asked for:

* Rooms with windows
* No more than 12 hours' work a day
* No night work
* Two suits of clothes a year
* Some education every day
* Girls and boys to be housed separately
* No more than two to share a bed

▲ Piecing and scavenging

▲ Factory children

The fact that the Act was passed indicates that conditions must have been harsh.

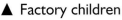

Birth of Josiah Wedgwood in Staffordshire	Begins work in family pottery	First business with capital of £20	Invented pyrometer: thermometer for kilns	Perfected black basalt unglazed stoneware	Perfected cameo ware	Invented jasper ware (Wedgwood blue)	Died worth £1.5 m
1730	1739	1759					1795

China teapots

Pottery, also a local craft, was transformed by the Industrial Revolution and the inventiveness and skills of an entrepreneur, Josiah Wedgwood.

How was it transformed?

Tea-drinking helped!

By 1765 it was estimated that nine out of ten families drank tea twice a day. People preferred to serve their tea using finer quality earthenware, rather than in ale mugs of pewter and heavy crockery.

It was discovered that if white Cornish clay was mixed with ground-up flint, a smoother china was produced. Wedgwood used this process to perfect his pottery, called creamware. He was so technically skilled that by experimenting and perfecting new glazes and firing techniques he was able, by the 1770s, to introduce six different types of ware.

▲ Creamware

Wedgwood's everyday china became so popular that he opened a new factory at Etruria near Stoke-on-Trent, with homes for workers nearby. Like Abraham Darby he used a Newcomen steam engine to pump water to work a waterwheel, and this powered the blast furnaces.

Wedgwood produced pottery in stages. His craftsmen specialised in one stage to improve their speed and skills. He employed about ten thousand workers.

▲ Wedgwood's London showroom, 1809

A partner looked after sales: he hired travelling salesmen, he advertised, he translated his catalogues into different languages for the European market and he opened showrooms.

After selling some creamware to the Queen Wedgwood was allowed to style himself 'Potter to Her Majesty' and call the creamware Queen's Ware. He gave money back to dissatisfied customers and replaced broken goods in transit. He demanded better transport for his fragile china and was prepared to fund new roads and back a new form of transport, canals.

Exeter Canal: By-passed weirs on River Exe	Newry Canal: Coal to port of Newry, Ireland	Sankey Brook made navigable from St Helen's coalfield to River Mersey	CANAL AGE BEGINS	Bridgewater Canal: Worsley to Manchester	Extension to Runcorn
1564	1724	1757		1761	1772–1776

CANALS

8

The canal age

Wedgwood wanted cheap transport to carry the raw material – clay – to his potteries, and to take the finished goods to the rest of England, and to the ports for export. The number of turnpiked roads was rapidly increasing, but road travel remained expensive and unsuitable for fragile china. River transport was vulnerable to flooding, drought and freezing.

One nearby landowner, the Duke of Bridgewater, wanted to make Worsley Brook, on his land, navigable for about 16 km between the Worsley collieries and Manchester. The cost of carrying tons of coal by packhorse made it too expensive to sell there.

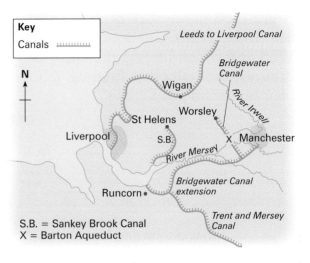

▲ The early canals around Manchester and Liverpool

A millwright, James Brindley, who worked for Wedgwood, was recommended to the Duke. In 1759 Brindley, who was almost illiterate, designed a canal with no locks, which tunnelled into coal mines, went over a bog and had a 'bridge' in the air. Critics scoffed. The Duke, who was considered insane, had huge difficulties mortgaging his land to raise money to finance the project. Within two years, however, the canal was completed and the price of Worsley coal was cut in half.

How was the cost cut?

One packhorse can carry about one-eighth of a tonne. One horse on a good road can pull a weight of about half a tonne. One horse on a canal side can pull a weight on water of up to 30 tonnes.

Between 1772 and 1776 Brindley built a 56 km extension to the Bridgewater Canal to meet the River Mersey at Runcorn. The cost of carrying cotton and cotton goods between Liverpool and Manchester was cut by five-sixths. The canal age had arrived.

▲ 'A bridge in the air': the revolutionary Barton Aqueduct over the River Irwell

43

James Brindley

Wedgwood made sure Brindley's next canal, the Grand Trunk (Trent and Mersey), begun in 1766 and which he and the Duke of Bridgewater helped to finance, made a detour past his factory at Etruria.

▲ The Grand Trunk Canal passes the Etruria factory

What did he gain?

Cornish clay was brought by sea to Chester or Liverpool and carried along the canal to Etruria. The fragile finished goods could travel by barge to Liverpool or Hull instead of being jolted by packhorse. Wedgwood's freight charges from Etruria to Manchester dropped from £2.75 per tonne to 75p per tonne.

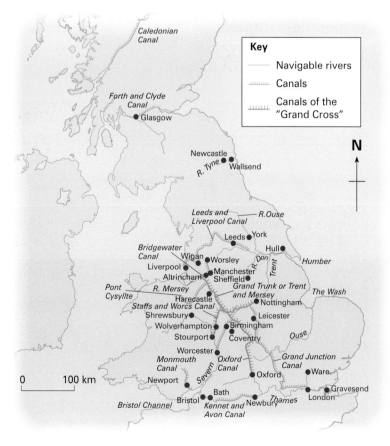

▲ Flowing water, still water: rivers and canals about 1795

When it was completed in 1777, this canal provided a continuous waterway across England from coast to coast, running 150 km from Runcorn to the River Trent.

To Brindley this was the first stage of a grand plan to link the major rivers Mersey, Trent, Severn and Thames by canal. The second stage was the Staffordshire and Worcestershire Canal which linked the Grand Trunk with the Severn via Wolverhampton, with a branch to Birmingham. The final stage of this 'Grand Cross', as it was called, was the Oxford Canal which linked the system with the Thames: this was completed in 1790.

Brindley also organised a force of 500 local farm labourers (navigators) and craftsmen. As the 'navvies' dug with pick and shovel, the craftsmen's forges and workshops would be floated along the canal following the work from place to place. By the time of Brindley's death in 1772 from overwork, his 'navvies' had dug 550 km of canal.

iron · marl · limestone · nails · corn · bills · letters · beer

timber · bricks · pottery · coal · cotton · fresh fruit and vegetables

Cargo for the barges

Canal construction

The construction of canals required considerable engineering ability and involved far more than digging a ditch. As the navvies became trained and experienced, they turned into skilled excavators. For obvious reasons, canals cannot slope! There were numerous technical problems to overcome to keep canals level:

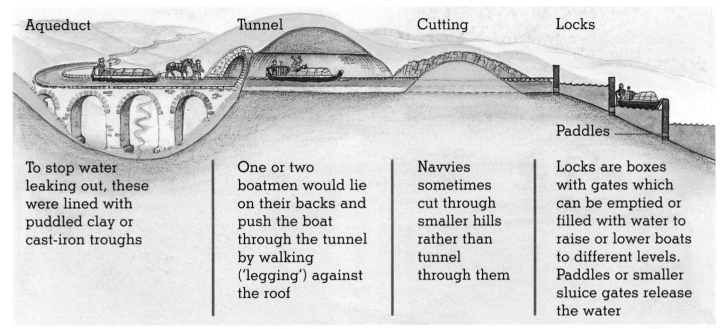

Aqueduct	Tunnel	Cutting	Locks
			Paddles
To stop water leaking out, these were lined with puddled clay or cast-iron troughs	One or two boatmen would lie on their backs and push the boat through the tunnel by walking ('legging') against the roof	Navvies sometimes cut through smaller hills rather than tunnel through them	Locks are boxes with gates which can be emptied or filled with water to raise or lower boats to different levels. Paddles or smaller sluice gates release the water

By 1815 the navvies had dug 2,200 miles of canals which changed the face of England.

Did industry benefit?

Enormously. Cheap transport of bulk goods such as iron and coal meant that industries could expand. Their productive capacity increased.

Areas such as the Midlands, which had been cut off from good cheap transport, now had a network of canals bringing raw materials to the factories. The population of areas such as the Potteries rose from 7,000 in 1760 to 20,000 by 1785.

▲ The canal, lock-gates, warehouses and boat-builders at Stourport, 1776

Canals also created new industrial sites. A new town, Stourport, was established where the Staffordshire and Worcestershire canal joined the River Severn.

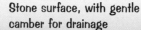 Narrow winding roads with sharp bends	Wide straight roads with no sharp bends	No proper surface or drainage	Stone surface, with gentle camber for drainage	Hump-back bridges, only wide enough for one-way traffic	Gently sloping bridges as wide as the road

Before and after turnpike trusts

Canal mania, turnpike fever

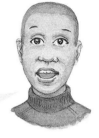

Was canal-building expensive?

Very. The Duke of Bridgewater estimated costs at £10,000 per mile. Even so, he and other investors made vast profits, and companies were able to pay dividends of 25 per cent to shareholders well into the nineteenth century.

Between 1791 and 1794, building started on forty-two canals at a total cost of £6 million. This led to a canal 'mania' when thousands rushed to buy shares. Some canals, however, built in non-industrial areas with locks that were too small, had little chance of making a profit. Costs were not met and investors lost money.

Canal and turnpike users both paid tolls. The difference was that turnpike trustees were not allowed to make a personal profit. They loaned money to receive interest.

So why did people finance trusts?

Landowners, merchants and manufacturers began to realise the benefits of improving roads to their farms and businesses.

▲ Turnpike roads, 1770

Population was increasing, industry was expanding and the demand for fresh food and goods was growing. Soon turnpiked roads spread like a rash over the face of the country.

By 1750, 146 turnpike trusts had been formed, managing about 5,500 km of highways. Over the next twenty years, during the turnpike 'fever', another forty were created, improving roads to meet the needs of an industrial nation.

▲ A mail coach setting out from London

In 1784 the first stagecoach service to carry mail was set up on the Bath–Bristol–London route. It was a great success in getting business correspondence more speedily around the country. The revolution in industry was thus matched by a revolution in transport.

46

William Small: Physician, mathematician, astronomer	Josiah Wedgwood: Ceramics	James Brindley: Hydraulics engineer	Erasmus Darwin: Physician, mechanics	Joseph Priestley: Experimental chemistry	Benjamin Franklin: American scientist and statesman	Members met when moon was full to see way home clearly

Members of the Lunar Society

The Lunar Society

STEAM
9
POWER

One fascinating by-product from the digging of canals into rock faces was the unearthing of fossil bones and shells.

Why was this of special interest?

A good friend and financial supporter of Wedgwood was his physician, Dr Erasmus Darwin. The canal findings stimulated one of his many interests, zoology, and gave him new ideas about the evolution of species. Wedgwood and Darwin were both members of the Lunar Society, based in Birmingham. Other members included scientists, inventors, astronomers, mathematicians, geologists, manufacturers and printers.

▲ The Bridgewater Canal at Worsley cut straight into the coal face

What was the purpose of the group?

Members met to discuss interesting issues of the time. They learnt from each other and were open to new ideas.

They experimented in electricity and chemistry in each other's homes. One famous member during his stay in Britain was the American statesman and scientist Benjamin Franklin who invented the lightning rod and bi-focal lenses. Another member was the ironmaster John Wilkinson. In 1779 he helped to build the first iron bridge; in 1787 he launched the first iron boat; he built a cast-iron Methodist chapel; put iron window frames, window sills and drainpipes on his own house; and was eventually buried in an iron coffin with an iron gravestone above.

Wilkinson's machines could accurately bore holes in cast-iron cylinders used for cannon, so he was able to help two other members, Matthew Boulton, an iron manufacturer, and James Watt, a Scottish engineer, with their experiments.

▲ James Watt studies a steam model of Newcomen's engine

First Boulton and Watt steam engine	'Up and down' motion	Pumped water at reservoirs, brine works, metal mines, breweries, distilleries	Raised water to turn wheels to operate bellows, forge-hammers and rolling-mills	Rotary motion invented	First used to work a hammer for John Wilkinson
1775				1781	1783

Boulton and Watt

In 1764 James Watt, an instrument-maker at Glasgow University, was asked to repair a model of the Newcomen engine (see page 8). Its one cylinder had to be heated and cooled, which wasted steam. Watt, recognising that this was inefficient, introduced a separate cylinder for condensing. He closed the top of the cylinder so the steam pushed the piston up and down.

To produce his machine, he went into partnership with John Roebuck of the Carron Ironworks at Glasgow. When Roebuck went bankrupt, Watt was invited to go into partnership with Matthew Boulton at his Soho works in Birmingham. Boulton's factory made the valves and small precision parts. John Wilkinson's machines bored the holes in the cylinders.

How successful was the new engine?

The first Boulton and Watt engine of 1775 used a quarter of the fuel of Newcomen's engine.

In 1781 Watt, helped by the foreman William Murdock, made a vital breakthrough in the progress of the Industrial Revolution. A cog attached to the rigid 'up and down' driving-rod slotted into a cog on the flywheel, forcing the wheel round. It was this rotary motion that was able to drive machinery of all kinds. Watt made further improvements, and by 1800 there were nearly 500 Boulton and Watt steam engines in use.

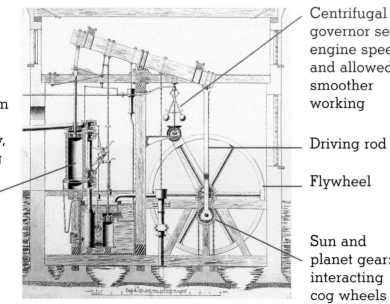

Steam injected into top and bottom cylinder alternately, increasing power output

Centrifugal governor set engine speed and allowed smoother working

Driving rod

Flywheel

Sun and planet gear: interacting cog wheels

▲ Watt's double-action steam engine, 1788

This machine, by replacing hand and muscle power in many industries, transformed the lives of hundreds of thousands of workers.

Spinning					Weaving			
2 cotton mills in Manchester	Watt's engine applied to spinning	Mills to move to towns	52 cotton mills in Manchester	4 out of 5 cotton goods are of mule yarn	Cartwright uses Watt engine to drive his power loom	2,400 power looms in use	14,000 power looms in use	100,000 power looms in use
1782	1785		1802	1811	1789	1813	1820	1833

The impact of steam

Did steam power mean the end of water power?

Not overnight! Water had the drawbacks of flooding, drought and freezing, but water-wheels, once installed, were cheap to run.

Better iron-making produced huge water-wheels and by 1800 they could generate 200 horsepower. The early steam engines generated about 20 horsepower.

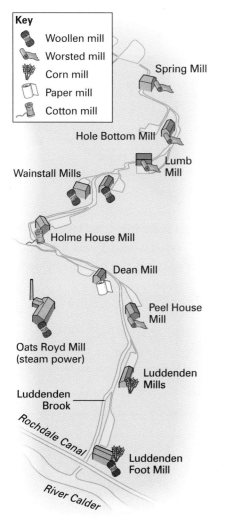

Key
- Woollen mill
- Worsted mill
- Corn mill
- Paper mill
- Cotton mill

Spring Mill
Hole Bottom Mill
Lumb Mill
Wainstall Mills
Holme House Mill
Dean Mill
Peel House Mill
Oats Royd Mill (steam power)
Luddenden Mills
Luddenden Brook
Rochdale Canal
Luddenden Foot Mill
River Calder

▲ Water power in the Luddenden valley around 1850

It was in the textile industries that steam power had its greatest impact. The first steam spinning mill was set up at Papplewick, Nottinghamshire, in 1785. As factory owners no longer needed to site their buildings near rivers, others were soon built in towns in Lancashire, Cheshire and Yorkshire.

In country areas, however, mill owners were wary of steam. Early steam engines were not very powerful or reliable, and there was a shortage of skilled labour to repair them. They therefore continued to build water-powered mills near strong-flowing rivers and reservoirs.

In the Luddenden valley, west of Halifax, Yorkshire, for example, the mills were served by three reservoirs maintained by the Cold Edge Dam Company. Raw materials and finished goods were shipped along the Rochdale Canal, which had been opened in 1804.

In 1847 however, when coal became cheap, the steam-powered Oats Royd woollen mill was built away from the water.

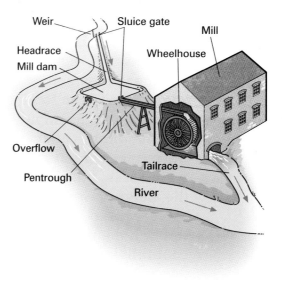

Weir
Sluice gate
Mill
Headrace
Mill dam
Wheelhouse
Overflow
Tailrace
Pentrough
River

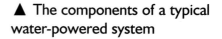

▲ The components of a typical water-powered system

The supremacy of steam

After 1850 the steam-powered Oats Royd mill expanded rapidly and became one of the largest worsted mills in the country. It began as a spinning mill, and power looms were originally housed in a mill nearby. When the company built multi-storied mills, space was provided for the power looms. Eventually a large weaving shed was built in 1887.

Combing followed a similar pattern. It began off-site and was done by hand. It was then sited in the first mill and a purpose-built shed (1858). It moved to a larger shed in 1885.

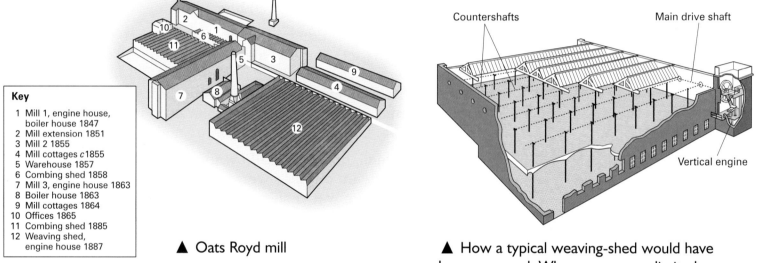

Key

1 Mill 1, engine house, boiler house 1847
2 Mill extension 1851
3 Mill 2 1855
4 Mill cottages c 1855
5 Warehouse 1857
6 Combing shed 1858
7 Mill 3, engine house 1863
8 Boiler house 1863
9 Mill cottages 1864
10 Offices 1865
11 Combing shed 1885
12 Weaving shed, engine house 1887

▲ Oats Royd mill

▲ How a typical weaving-shed would have been powered. Where space was limited a vertical engine replaced the beam engine

Many other factors apart from steam – such as changes in fashion, competition from foreign markets and the supply of raw materials – affected the success of individual businesses, but owners of the water-powered mills soon realised that only through the use of steam could their mills generate enough power to expand.

By the late nineteenth century steam had become the dominant source of power.

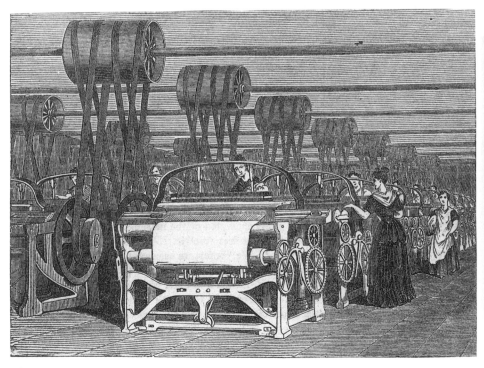

▲ The sort of power loom used at Oats Royd mill, about 1840

Birth of Richard Trevithick Son of Cornish mining engineer	Steam road carriage Holborn to Paddington	Steam locomotive	'Catch-me-who-can'	Improved steam engines in Peruvian mines	Moved to Costa Rica	Returned to England – employed by Robert Stephenson	Died in poverty
1771	1803	1804	1808	1816	1822	1827	1833

'Catch me' at 16 km per hour

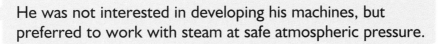

Did Watt think of the possibility of steam-powered transport?

He was not interested in developing his machines, but preferred to work with steam at safe atmospheric pressure.

William Murdock built a working model of a high-pressure steam locomotive in 1784, but the company told him to focus on stationary machines rather than 'idle dreams'.

It was Richard Trevithick, a former pupil of Murdock, who patented a high-pressure steam engine. It did not need a beam or condenser because the piston was driven by 'strong-steam'. This steam, about three times atmospheric pressure, did not burst the boiler, used less fuel, and was light enough to be carried in a cart.

After experiments with road steam carriages, Trevithick thought of building a railway locomotive. On February 21 1804, at the Pen-y-darren Ironworks, Merthyr Tydfil, a Trevithick locomotive drew five wagons, a coach and about seventy passengers to the Glamorgan Canal, 16 km away.

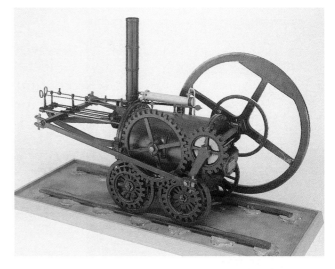

▲ The Pen-y-darren locomotive

How fast was it, and how long did it take?

It reached a top speed of 8 km per hour and took four hours!

This was because the locomotive, weighing 5 tonnes, cracked the iron tramways in places. Nevertheless, it was an historic journey.

In 1808 Trevithick opened a public railway running on a circular track near Euston, London. Called the 'Catch-me-who-can', it carried the first fare-paying passengers at a shilling a ride and reached 16 km per hour.

Like some of his other ventures in life, however, it failed financially and was withdrawn. Though Trevithick was the inventor of effective steam locomotion, others benefited from his pioneering work.

▲ The 'Catch-me-who-can'

Coke smelting for cast iron	Improved coke smelting for wrought iron	Houses for workers
Quaker and pacifist	6 new blast furnaces	High wages
	Bought iron ore and coal mines	Bought local farms for
	Used steam pumps and horse-drawn	food for workers
	wagonway	Ironbridge
1677–1717 Abraham Darby I	**1711–1763** Abraham Darby II	**1750–1791** Abraham Darby III

Coalbrookdale

Where was the iron produced for the machines, the water-wheels, the engines, the tools and the nails?

Coalbrookdale was at the heart of the iron industry and has often been referred to as the birthplace of the Industrial Revolution.

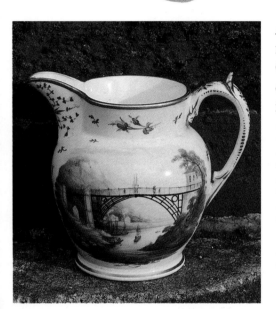

▲ Ironbridge pictured on a Coalport jug of 1836

Abraham Darby II developed his father's work, and in 1750 managed to smelt pig iron with coke to produce wrought iron. Once this more supple iron could be made on a large scale, iron continued to pour out of the blast furnaces there. Many iron inventions were 'born' at Coalbrookdale.

1707 – Casting of iron cooking-pots in sand-moulds

1711 – Cast-iron cylinders for Newcomen's steam engines

1729 – First iron wheels for wagonways

1767 – First iron plate rails with flanges to replace wooden rails on wagonways

1778 – Boulton and Watt's steam engines made under licence here: Abraham Darby III bought one to work the bellows for blast furnaces

1779 – Ironbridge built

1802 – First steam locomotives built for Trevithick

1800s – Telford, an engineer, had cast-iron troughs and parts for his aqueducts built here

Coalbrookdale needed good transport links. Horses brought coal in by wagons on railways from the mines. The first iron bridge built by John Wilkinson in partnership with Abraham Darby III was to make the fetching of timber and limestone easier. The canal system came in 1788 and a turnpiked road was built in 1817. The Darby family, over the eighteenth century, adapted to each stage of industrial demand.

▲ Coalbrookdale in 1801: an awesome sight. The Industrial Revolution changed the face of the English landscape

Seven Years' War	Wilkinson built cannon at Broseley works	Roebuck's works at Carron beside River Clyde	Guest's works at Dowlais, South Wales	Crawshay's Cyfartha works at Merthyr Tydfil	Merthyr had 6 blast furnaces, 2 rolling mills, 4 steam engines, employed 2,000, produced 200 tonnes of iron per week
1756–1763		1759	1759	1760s	1790s

More iron

The Darbys, as Quakers and pacifists, did not set up munitions factories, but other ironmasters did, especially during the Seven Years' War against France. One ironmaster, Henry Cort, had a forge near Portsmouth and was under contract to the Admiralty to supply wrought-iron goods to the Royal Navy.

The forging of bar (wrought) iron was slow in comparison with the mass production of pig (cast) iron. Converting pig iron to bar iron still required charcoal and heating and hammering to remove impurities. In 1783 and 1784 Cort introduced two new processes, 'puddling' and 'rolling'.

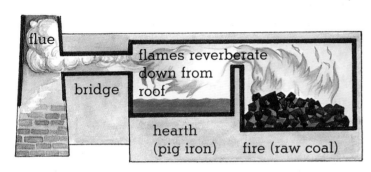

▲ The reverberatory furnace

During puddling the coal in the furnace was separated from the pig iron by a bridge. Flames from the fire swept over the bridge and bounced down (reverberated) from the roof onto the pig iron. The puddler stirred (puddled) the molten iron until much of the carbon and impurities had been burnt away. He then formed the purified spongy iron into balls. These were taken out with tongs and passed between grooved iron rollers which removed further impurities. Iron, after rolling, became as supple as leather.

Did this mean charcoal was no longer needed to make wrought iron?

▲ Rollers and puddling furnace at Cyfartha ironworks

Yes, and now forges could move near to furnaces in coalfields.

Soon the industry became concentrated in four main areas – Staffordshire, South Yorkshire, the Clyde and South Wales. New communities, with dense populations, grew up. The output of iron increased vastly.

By 1800 Britain was producing more iron than the rest of the world put together. She needed this iron, particularly for the French Revolutionary War which started in 1793.

French Revolution	Constituent Assembly	Storming of Bastille	Declaration of 'Rights of Man'	Execution of Louis XVI	France declares war on Britain	Coalition of 14 states including Britain, Austria, Prussia, Holland, Spain, Portugal, Sardinia, Papal States
	1789 July 9	July 14	August 26	1793 January 21	February	1792–1797

WAR WITH FRANCE 11

America and the French Revolution

How were these revolutions connected?

In 1778 France had entered the American War of Independence on the side of the rebels, and helped them to defeat Britain. This war had two effects on France.

▲ The French general Lafayette meets George Washington

First, the costs had proved crippling and France was approaching bankruptcy. To pay for the war the government increased taxes, but the nobles and higher clergy were not required to pay more. The burden fell on the merchants, manufacturers and peasants, who were already heavily taxed. These taxes, plus high prices for bread and a growing resentment at the extravagances of the court of Louis XVI, fuelled discontent.

Second, the ideals of the Declaration of Independence appealed to writers and thinkers in France who thought that French people, too, should have basic rights such as freedom of speech and governments that ruled with the consent of the people. Louis XVI resisted attempts to limit his powers, but in a revolution of unforeseen and often incomprehensible violence and bloodshed, the French people secured a constitutional government and their famous basic rights of 'liberté, égalité, fraternité'.

Thousands of nobles (émigrés) fled almost certain death at the hands of the Revolutionary government and urged the monarchs of Europe to help them put down the Revolution. In April 1792 the Revolutionary government retaliated by declaring war on Austria and Prussia. In January 1793 Louis XVI was guillotined and French troops occupied Belgium.

In February 1793 war was declared against Britain and Holland. Britain joined a coalition, a military union of fourteen states, but in 1797, when this first coalition was defeated, Britain stood alone against France.

▲ The execution of Louis XVI

Ireland: Share king, Parliament, army	100 MPs in Commons, 28 peers, 4 bishops in Lords	Church of Ireland joined with Church of England	Judiciary and laws unchanged	Free trade between Britain and Ireland	Share trade privileges in empire	

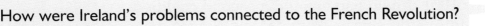

1801 January, Union with Ireland

The new Union Jack

Ireland and the French Revolution

How were Ireland's problems connected to the French Revolution?

The ideals of liberty, equality and fraternity appealed to many in Ireland, as they had to some in Britain.

In 1791 a Society of United Irishmen of young Protestants, Catholics and Presbyterians was formed under the leadership of Wolfe Tone. While England was preoccupied with war, Tone persuaded the French to raise an invasion force to land in Ireland.

In December 1796 thirteen French ships, with 14,000 troops, were prevented from landing by storms and fog. A second attempt with Dutch help failed when the British defeated it near Camperdown. Three more French expeditions failed. Then Tone was arrested and committed suicide. Pitt, the Prime Minister, realised that if the French had secured a base in Ireland, it could have altered the course of the war. Putting Britain's security first, he pushed for a political union with Ireland.

Pitt genuinely wanted Catholic emancipation (freedom) and a weakening of the 'Protestant ascendancy'. So that a union could take place, members of the Irish Parliament were offered peerages, pensions, jobs and money payments to vote for its own end. Once these were accepted, the Act of Union went ahead in 1801. Under this, the two countries shared the same king, Parliament and army. Trade restrictions were lifted. One hundred Irish MPs sat in the Commons, and twenty-eight Irish peers and four bishops in the Lords.

▲ The Irish Parliament, 1782

Did the Union please the Irish?

No, because Pitt had given only a 'gentleman's agreement' that Catholic emancipation would follow.

George III blocked this, and Pitt, realising that a Union in which Irish Catholics were represented by Protestant MPs would not work, resigned. Catholics felt betrayed, and tensions between Britain and Ireland continued.

Birth of Horatio Nelson	Joins Navy	First captaincy	Loses sight of right eye, Corsica	Loses right arm in attack on Tenerife	Battle of Nile, Nelson's greatest victory	Battle of Copenhagen, telescope to blind eye	Commander-in-chief, Mediterranean	Death at Trafalgar	Nelson's Column, Trafalgar Square
1759	1771	1779	1794	1797	1798	1801	1803	1805 Oct 21	1843

Boney will get you!

By 1801 Britain had entered a second coalition with Austria, Russia, Portugal and Naples, but now faced a French general of genius, Napoleon Bonaparte. Soon, after a string of French victories, Britain once more stood alone.

A peace treaty was signed with France in 1802, but in 1804 Napoleon declared himself Emperor of France and decided on an invasion of Britain. He placed 100,000 troops of his Grand Army, which had defeated every continental force, ready at Calais. He assembled 2,000 flat-bottomed barges and flotillas of smaller armed vessels, ready to attack patrolling British frigates.

▲ The Great Invasion Scare, 1804–1805

How did Britain defend herself?

She had 52,000 regular troops, 120,000 county militia forces who needed training, and 350,000 men in part-time volunteer regiments, some with neither weapons nor training.

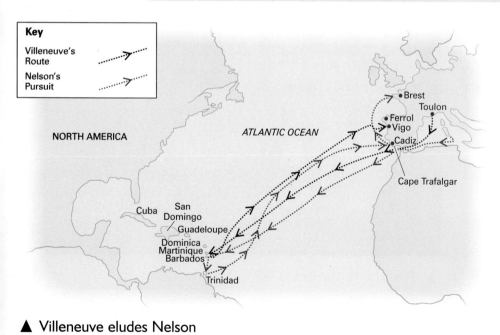

Key
Villeneuve's Route
Nelson's Pursuit

NORTH AMERICA
ATLANTIC OCEAN
Brest
Toulon
Ferrol
Vigo
Cadiz
Cape Trafalgar
Cuba
San Domingo
Guadeloupe
Dominica
Martinique
Barbados
Trinidad

▲ Villeneuve eludes Nelson

If London was attacked, George III was determined to lead the defending troops. Martello towers were built along the south-east coast, and semaphores and beacons were set up on hill-tops. Artillery and stores from Woolwich Arsenal were to be taken by canal to the Midlands.

Napoleon could not transport his troops over in one night, so he ordered the French fleet under Villeneuve to elude a blockade near Toulon, entice the British fleet under Nelson to the West Indies, and double back to protect the invasion barges.

Villeneuve eluded the blockade but put in at Cadiz to re-fit. In August 1805 Napoleon moved the Grand Army from Calais to face a third coalition and ordered Villeneuve back to the Mediterranean in support. Nelson, Commander-in-chief in the Mediterranean, waited with his fleet outside Cadiz for the French fleet to emerge.

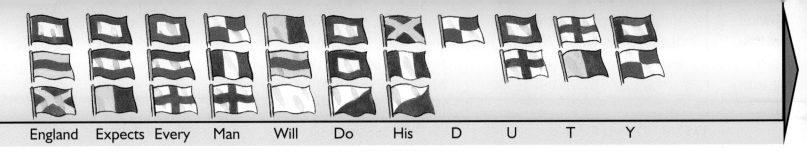

Nelson at Trafalgar

On October 21 1805, at 5.50 am, the combined French and Spanish fleet under Villeneuve was sighted ten miles away between the English fleet and the coast of Trafalgar. Nelson had already planned his tactics. The usual battle plan was to sail alongside the enemy in a parallel line and fire on a marked opponent.

6.00 am – Nelson signals fleet to form two columns. These are ready to sail at right angles to cut off leading enemy ships.

11.50 am – Villeneuve signals fleet to open fire as soon as English are in range. Nelson signals: 'England expects every man will do his duty'.

12.00 pm – *Royal Sovereign* goes under fire.

12.10 pm – *Royal Sovereign* fires broadside at *Santa Ana* at point-blank range.

▲ The fleets at 12 noon

12.30 pm – First broadsides strike at *Victory*, still a mile from enemy.

1.00 pm – *Victory* engages *Bucentaure*. Over 200 grenades land on *Victory*'s decks.

1.15 pm – Nelson struck in left shoulder by sniper's musket bullet.

1.30 pm – *Victory* crashes into *Redoutable*. *Téméraire* comes to its aid.

2.05 pm – Villeneuve surrenders *Bucentaure*.

2.30 pm – Lucas surrenders *Redoutable* to *Victory*.

4.30 pm – Nelson dies, knowing of the success: 'Thank God I have done my duty.'

5.20 pm – Last shots of battle fired.

Of twenty-seven English ships, none is lost. Of thirty-three French and Spanish ships, fifteen are sunk, blown up or run ashore, eight are taken as prizes and ten limp back to Calais. About 1,700 British and 7,000 French and Spanish sailors are killed or wounded.

What did victory achieve?

With the French fleet destroyed, Napoleon could not plan for another invasion of Britain.

▲ In the heat of the battle

Main battles (and victors)	Valmy, Sept 1792 (Fr) Jemappes, Nov 1792 (Fr) Rivoli, Jan 1797 (Fr)	Pyramids, July 1798 (Fr) Nile, Aug 1798 (Br) Aboukir, July 1799 (Fr) Marengo, June 1800 (Fr) Hohenlinden, Dec 1800 (Fr)	Ulm, Oct 1805 (Fr) Trafalgar, Oct 1805 (Br) Austerlitz, Dec 1805 (Fr)
	1792–1797 First Coalition	**1798–1801** Second Coalition	**1803–1805** Third Coalition

The Continental System

A STOPPAGE to a STRIDE over the GLOBE

▲ Napoleon astride the globe

The day before Trafalgar, Napoleon's Grand Army had defeated Austria at Ulm and he went on to win an amazing sequence of battles during the period of the Third Coalition.

Napoleon now aimed to defeat Britain by the use of economic warfare. His weapon was the Continental System. If he could stop Britain selling goods to Europe and importing corn, her debts would increase, her credit would be undermined, and she would be unable to form further coalitions against him. In 1806 he issued his Berlin decrees. All continental ports had to be closed to English shipping.

What could Britain do?

Retaliate.

In the Orders of Council of 1807, all ships which came from a French or European port controlled by Napoleon would be seized. Ships from neutral countries would have to pay a duty at a British port before trading with a country in Europe.

Napoleon replied with his Milan Decree of 1807. Any ship obeying the Orders of Council would be seized. A further decree ordered that seized British goods were to be burnt in public.

Did the system work?

There was certainly hardship when imports and exports were blocked.

▲ The burning of British goods by French troops

Unemployment and high bread prices, especially after bad harvests, caused food riots. Britain even went to war with the USA from 1812 to 1814 over interference with her trade which interrupted supplies of raw cotton.

France and other countries needed British goods and colonial produce, and Napoleon could not prevent smuggling, which was highly organised. In 1812 he removed the embargo.

New European 'royal family' of Bonaparte				Belgium and Netherlands part of French empire	New Kingdom of Italy	Grand Duchy of Warsaw: once belonged to Prussia	Protector of Confederation of Rhineland
Louis (brother) King of Holland	Joseph (brother) King of Naples	Jérôme (brother) King of Westphalia	Joseph King of Spain				
1806	1806	1807	1808	1811			

Wellington at Waterloo

By 1811 Napoleon was master of Europe, but it was by trying to enforce the Continental System on countries such as Portugal, Spain and Russia – who were still trading with Britain – that led him into wars he could not win.

In 1808 Britain had landed troops in Portugal, and in 1813, under the Duke of Wellington, British forces drove Napoleon's troops out of Spain. In Russia, Napoleon entered Moscow in 1812, but facing winter without any communication from the Czar over peace terms, his troops withdrew. Thousands died in the retreat. On his return, Napoleon was defeated by the forces of a Sixth Coalition at Leipzig, captured and banished to Elba, an island off the Italian coast.

In February 1815 he escaped and assembled an army to confront Wellington's allied army at Waterloo in Belgium. Napoleon, with 71,947 men and 246 guns, was confident of victory against Wellington's 67,661 men and 156 guns. This ten-hour battle, fought in mud, was a terrible one. Combined losses were more than 74,000 men. The arrival of the Prussian army under Blücher, just as Wellington was facing defeat, swung the balance in favour of Britain. Wellington said that the victory was 'the nearest run thing you ever saw'.

Napoleon was exiled to St Helena, an island in the South Atlantic, and died there in 1821.

▲ The Battle of Waterloo

Why was the Battle of Waterloo so important?

It proved to be one of the turning-points of history. It marked the end of the period of the French Revolution and the era of Napoleon. It ushered in a period of almost forty years of peace in Europe.

Price of a large loaf \ Size of family	Single man	Single woman	Man and wife	With one child	With two children
1s 0d	3s 0d	2s 0d	4s 6d	6s 0d	7s 6d
1s 1d	3s 3d	2s 1d	4s 10d	6s 5d	8s 0d

Example:
A man earns 7 shillings a week. A loaf of bread is 1s 1d. He is married with two children. Allowance will be 1s 0d to make 8s 0d.

Speenhamland table of allowances

The Speenhamland system

Even before the Continental System was imposed, the deliveries of imported corn during the French wars were erratic. Britain needed more corn, especially after poor harvests, and whenever corn was in short supply, prices rose. There was also a rapid increase in Parliamentary Enclosure Acts at this time.

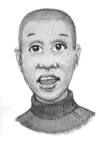

Why?

Farmers who enclosed fields to concentrate on large-scale production of corn, made large profits when corn became scarce.

High prices for bread, together with low wages, meant that agricultural labourers often existed at starvation level.

In 1795 magistrates in Speenhamland, near Newbury, Berkshire, held a meeting to discuss what to do about poverty in their county. They decided, as well as continuing with poor relief for the elderly and sick, to supplement inadequate wages with an 'allowance'. This was calculated on the man's wage, the size of his family, and the price of a loaf of bread. This 'bread money', as the poor called it, at last meant that they need not starve.

The 'Speenhamland' system was quickly adopted by other parishes in the south.

▲ A farm labourer receives his wages from the landowner

But if the parish always paid an allowance, the farmers need not pay higher wages ...

This is what happened. The agricultural labourer, no matter how hard he worked, rarely earned more. The idle worker could claim the same allowance.

Genuine hard-working labourers, who had never applied for assistance from the parish before, felt humiliated at having to do so now. Critics argued that some poor people deliberately had larger families so they could claim more allowance.

The poor rates increased and some farmers became poorer. The problem of poverty was still not solved.

Ned Ludd:
Said to be an apprentice living in
Sherwood Forest –
probably a false name to protect identities

Great Enoch:
Large sledgehammer used by Luddites,
made by Enoch Taylor
of Marsden,
West Yorkshire

1811

Ned Ludd and the Luddites

Not only agricultural workers suffered during the Napoleonic Wars.
When the price of corn rose, and supplies of raw materials were
uncertain, unemployment and hardship affected other workers too.
Some, known as Luddites, decided to act.

Who were the Luddites?

These were skilled men, the handloom weavers, the shearers and
croppers, who were fighting to keep their work.

But the textile mills, which established mass-
production of goods with their water- and steam-
powered machines, required fewer, lower-paid and
unskilled workers. Mills had been destroyed before,
but Luddite attacks were better planned, disciplined
and more violent. Warning letters from the
mysterious Ned Ludd made the intent clear.

There were such serious disturbances in the North
and Midlands that 12,000 troops, the largest number
ever used to quell a local disturbance, were
stationed in those areas. Their job was difficult as
the Luddites had support and remained well
concealed.

In 1811, in Nottingham and Derbyshire the machine-
breakers attacked the wide stocking-frames which
produced cheap, inferior stockings. In Lancashire
several thousand workers, including colliers,
attacked Burton's power-loom mill at Middleton. Five
rioters were killed by musket fire. In Yorkshire,
croppers and shearers attacked the gig-mills and
shearing-frames.

This was a violent campaign which culminated in
the murder of an unpopular factory-owner. In 1812
machine-breaking became a capital offence. In that
year, seventeen Luddites were hanged at York and
others transported.

The government, fearful of riots like those of the
French Revolution, now clamped down hard on the
workers.

Sir

*Information has just been given that you
are a holder of those detestable shearing-
frames and I was asked by my men to
write to you and give fair warning to pull
them down. If they are not taken down by
the end of the week I shall send at least
300 men to destroy them.*

Signed, Ned Ludd

▲ Luddite letter sent to a mill-owner

▲ The end of teasels: a 'gig-mill'
to raise the nap of woollen cloth

Corn Bill: Protests in newspapers, pamphlets and meetings	First reading of Bill	Protests from humanitarians, manufacturers, Poor Law overseers	Estimated crowd of 10,000–20,000 dispersed	Attacks on houses of Corn Law supporters	One petition reaches 42,473 signatures	Corn Laws passed
1814	1815 March		March 6	March 7	March 10	March 23

The Corn Laws

Protests continued after the wars and not all were confined to the poor. The merchants and manufacturers protested too when the Corn Bill was read in Parliament.

What were they protesting against?

The landowners, particularly those who had enclosed their fields and made huge profits from growing more corn, did not want foreign imports to resume and threaten their wealth.

They argued that Britain should not have to depend on other countries for their food, and that food prices could be kept stable. Profits could be invested in farming, and agriculture would benefit. Competition between different areas to see who could produce the most wheat would also be beneficial.

In 1815 these wealthy landowners – who formed the bulk of MPs in the Commons and Lords – persuaded Parliament to pass the Corn Laws. These stated that corn could only be imported when the average prices of home-grown corn were at or above 80s (£4) per quarter (about 200 kg) for wheat and at or above 40s (£2) per quarter for barley. If prices fell below those levels, no foreign corn, meal or flour could be imported.

Did prices fall?

Yes, corn rarely reached the 80 shilling level.

The factory-owners resented the landowners being favoured at the expense of others. They complained that if the price of bread rose, they would have to pay workers more. This would increase the price of their goods, they would sell less, and be able to employ fewer people.

The workers protested as they would struggle to make ends meet. There were petitions and riots. 'No Corn Bill!', 'No starvation!', 'No landlords!' were the cries.

▲ An anti-Corn Law cartoon of 1815

Hampden and Union clubs campaign for reform	Spa Fields Riots	Game Law: 7 years' imprisonment for anyone found with net	March of 'Blanketeers'	Prince Regent's coach attacked	Habeas Corpus Act suspended: Troublemakers imprisoned without trial	1,500 petitions for reform
1816	1816	1817	1817	1817		1818

The Peterloo Massacre

The government tended to view mass meetings over low wages and high prices as part of a gigantic plot to promote a French form of revolution. Troops were often used to keep order.

But manufacturers, the gentry and working men began to hold meetings, present petitions and write articles to push for a reform of Parliament itself. They demanded universal suffrage – that is, one man, one vote.

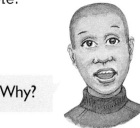

Why?

▲ The Peterloo Massacre

They felt that only when MPs were fairly elected as representatives of the people could changes be made to improve society.

These reformers, particularly the educated working men, thought that the government would listen to them if they could show that the public supported them. One meeting took place on August 16 1819 at St Peter's Fields, Manchester. The crowd of about 6,000 unarmed and orderly men, women and children, some holding banners demanding 'Votes for All' and 'A Free Press', had assembled to listen to a well-known speaker on reform, Henry Hunt.

The meeting began, but the magistrates, alarmed at the size of the crowd, sent in the Manchester and Cheshire yeomanry to arrest Hunt. The horsemen were shouted at and hustled by the crowd, so the magistrates ordered the cavalry, held in reserve, to charge. The resulting panic ended in eleven deaths, including two women, over a hundred wounded, and several hundred injured by horses' hooves.

The magistrates were thanked by the Prince Regent and the Home Secretary. Hunt was gaoled for two years and Parliament rushed through six new acts. The public were shocked that troops who had fought a tyrant at Waterloo should be used against fellow countrymen in this way. The incident became known sarcastically as 'Peterloo'.

Possession of arms prohibited	Marching and weapon practice banned	Public meetings of over 50 banned	Increase of duty on pamphlets made them too expensive to buy	Magistrates could search homes for literature attacking Church or government	Magistrates could try cases previously tried by judge and jury

1819 The 'Six Acts'

The Cato Street Conspiracy

What did the 'Six Acts' do?

They tried to stifle any attempts for reform by:

- giving magistrates powers to search houses for arms
- forbidding military training in private
- forbidding meetings of over 50 people without magistrates' consent
- increasing stamp duty on newspapers and political pamphlets
- making publishers of seditious libel, such as attacks on government, liable to transportation
- speeding up trial procedure.

Although not harshly applied, the measures were approved by many in Parliament, especially when, in the following February, a plot to assassinate the whole Cabinet was uncovered.

The leader of the conspiracy, Arthur Thistlewood, was already known to the government through his involvement in other plots. His group was infiltrated by a government spy, George Edwards, the plans were reported and the group was arrested while assembling at their Cato Street headquarters in London. During the arrest, Thistlewood stabbed and killed a Bow Street Runner. He and four others were convicted of high treason and sentenced to be hanged, beheaded and quartered. It was the last public decapitation in Britain, although the last part of the sentence was not carried out. The informer Edwards was hounded out of the country.

▲ The rights of a free-born Englishman are mocked in an 1819 cartoon

After 1820, as trade improved and unemployment declined, discontent did lessen. The powers of magistrates to search for arms, however, continued for two years, and the ban on public meetings lasted for five years. Some reforms, demanded by the changing social and economic conditions, were required. Those involving law and order were long overdue.

▲ The arrest of the Cato Street conspirators, February 23 1820

Population of London over 1 million	11,300 Stepney people made homeless when St Katherine's Dock is built	The word 'slum' dates from the 1820s	'As well to be hanged for a sheep as a lamb': Proverb of the time	Population of London grows to about 2 million
1801	1828			1851

Law and order

What were the Bow Street Runners?

An early police force set up in 1748 at Bow Street, London, by a magistrate, Henry Fielding.

The original Runners were a group of parish constables who were unpaid but earned money if those they arrested were successfully prosecuted. They also made a living by acting as private detectives.

After Fielding's death in 1754, his half-brother, the blind magistrate John Fielding, carried on his work and introduced uniformed horse- and foot-patrols. In 1792 the success of his scheme led Parliament to set up seven more police offices, each with three magistrates and six constables.

In 1800 another office was set up to deal with crime on the River Thames. Here, acres of land had been cleared to build warehouses for the London docks. Homeless people moved into districts nearby which rapidly became overcrowded slums.

Apart from the Runners, only unpaid constables and paid night-watchmen – old men who were easily bribed or threatened – enforced the law. Criminal behaviour was commonplace in a capital where the population was growing and where the chances of being caught were slim.

Punishments were severe. By 1820 about 160 crimes were capital offences. These included the theft of goods worth more than forty shillings, housebreaking, sheep-stealing, scribbling on Westminster Bridge and digging up a tree in Downing Street!

Many judges and juries found the defendants 'not guilty', rather than let them hang for a minor offence. Juries would swear goods taken by a prisoner were worth thirty-nine, not forty, shillings, and so save an individual from the gallows. The law was clearly being brought into disrepute.

▲ Public executions were a fairly common spectacle

4,500 thieves and robbers	2,700 disturbers of peace, drunks, brawlers, etc.	800 pickpockets	1,000 vagrants, tramps and travelling homeless people	400 frauds, con-men, street criminals	5,800 prostitutes

1837 London police record of crimes and criminals

Police reform

There had been earlier unsuccessful campaigns to abolish the death penalty for most crimes, but in 1823 Robert Peel, then Home Secretary, persuaded Parliament to change the law. Judges could now impose reduced sentences for crimes that did not involve killing. By 1838 people in Britain could be hanged only for treason and murder.

Peel also wanted to set up a properly organised police force.

Did Londoners want this?

There was resistance. Many felt a police force would be a threat to an Englishman's freedom – whereas criminals were not considered to be so!

The government, though, still feared a revolution of the French kind, which had begun in the slums of Paris. Others recognised that the lives and property of rich and poor should be protected. A need was felt for a disciplined force, but not a military one.

In 1829 Peel's Metropolitan Police Improvement Bill became law. 3,314 constables ('bobbies') were recruited, under overall charge of two commissioners.

The idea was to prevent crime by their visible presence on the streets. Each constable patrolled his 'beat'. This meant 30 km of walking a day, seven days a week. Discipline was severe, and many early recruits were dismissed for drunkenness. London, with its open sewers, impure water and terrible winter fogs caused by smoky coal fires, was unhealthy. Many policemen died of tuberculosis or became unfit for duty.

By acting with restraint, the police gradually became accepted by most of the general public. The Metropolitan Police became the model for all provincial borough forces. In 1856 it became compulsory for all counties to have a police force.

Peel also ended the detested system of paid government spies – 'agents provocateurs' – who provoked incidents to trigger arrests.

▲ Cartoon of a 'peeler' or 'bobby', 1829

Prison reform

When Peel turned to prison reform, he found much to change.

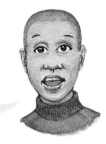

Were prisons overcrowded?

Yes, but not with criminals!

Very few people were in prison as a punishment. Debtors, for example, would be sent to gaol, along with people waiting to be tried. Others who had been found guilty waited there for punishments such as hanging, flogging, the stocks or pillory.

There were different sorts of gaols – county, town, private ones and some called Bridewells, or houses of correction, for homeless vagrants. The prison governor, the gaoler, received no salary but charged fees – for admission, release, putting on and taking off irons.

Prisoners found innocent, who could not afford the fees, stayed inside. Those with money could rent a bed, and eat and drink well. Those without means lived on public money of 2d a day, which provided a pound of bread.

Children, men and women, innocent and guilty, could all be held together. Disease, particularly typhus (gaol fever), spread quickly.

Two notable early reformers were John Howard, an evangelical Christian, and Elizabeth Fry, a nonconformist Quaker. Peel accepted their harrowing evidence to produce a Gaols Act of 1823. Under this:

- Gaols had to be secure and healthy
- Gaolers were to be paid by the government
- Magistrates were to visit prisons
- Women prisoners were to be kept separate from men and have female warders
- Surgeons and chaplains had to visit regularly
- Teachers were employed
- Attempts had to be made to reform prisoners.

▲ Prison ships ('hulks') for those awaiting transportation. These relieved overcrowded prisons

67

Peel's Gaols Act	Silent and separate systems based on American schemes	Millbank Prison opened	Pentonville Prison opened	Dartmoor Prison, used for French prisoners of war, opened as state prison	Prison Act: Separate cells for all prisoners Punishment cells or flogging Solitary confinement for 3 days and nights on bread and water
1823	1841	1842	1850		1865

Silent or separate

What attempts were made to reform prisoners?

Two ideas were tried: the silent system and the separate system.

The silent system involved hard or monotonous labour undertaken in complete silence so prisoners could not corrupt each other. The treadwheel, or 'everlasting staircase' (as convicts called it), was like the wheel in a hamster's cage. Men stood at the top, and as they trod down, the steps beneath them fell away.

The crank was like an old-fashioned mangle. As prisoners turned the handle, a box scooped up and emptied cups of sand. After several thousand turns were recorded on the meter, the prisoner earned his meal.

Oakum-picking (unravelling old rope to make doormats) was a dreary task which made fingers red and raw.

The separate system was solitary confinement in the prisoner's own cell. When the hardened criminal's spirit was broken after days of enforced solitude, the chaplain persuaded him to lead a better, more godly life. Solitary confinement was the policy in the new Pentonville Prison, opened in 1842. It was clean and well planned, but the suicide rates were higher than in any of the older gaols.

▲ Oakum-picking and treadwheel

After 1852 Australia refused to accept any more convicts. More British prisons were opened and transportation was replaced by penal servitude.

Under this system, eighteen months were spent in solitary confinement. This was followed by work in some sort of public works scheme; if behaviour was good, a 'ticket of leave' was granted. The prisoner left gaol but was bound by restrictions such as having to report to a local police station.

By the 1850s the foundations of the modern police force and prison services had been laid.

John Metcalfe: Blind from the age of six Constructed 320 km of roads in Yorks. and Lancs.	John Loudon McAdam: Son of Scottish engineer	Tarmac(adam): Word comes from the time when roads were covered with bitumen (tar)	Thomas Telford: Son of Scottish shepherd First president of Institution of Civil Engineers
1717–1810	1756–1836		1757–1834

Road improvements

During and after the Napoleonic Wars, turnpike trusts had continued apace, particularly near the ports in Kent, the coalfields in the North-east and the cotton factories in Lancashire. More wheeled traffic on the roads meant that surfaces became damaged, so the trusts employed engineers to maintain and build new roads.

One early self-taught engineer was John Metcalfe (Blind Jack of Knaresborough) who could judge the state of the roads by tapping with his stick. His solutions included using bundles of heather with stone above and a surface of gravel cambered (curved) to carry off surface water into ditches alongside.

Two great engineers of the later turnpike era were Scotsmen. They both considered drainage and gentle gradients to be important.

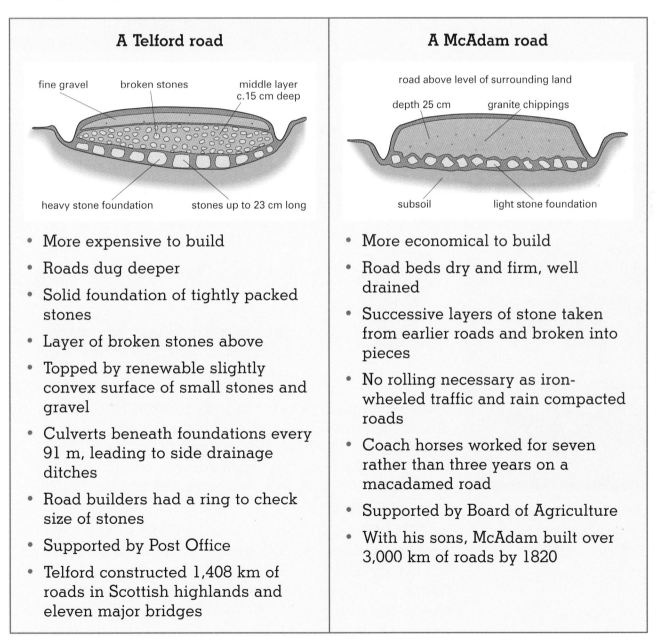

A Telford road	A McAdam road
fine gravel, broken stones, middle layer c.15 cm deep, heavy stone foundation, stones up to 23 cm long	*road above level of surrounding land, depth 25 cm, granite chippings, subsoil, light stone foundation*

A Telford road

- More expensive to build
- Roads dug deeper
- Solid foundation of tightly packed stones
- Layer of broken stones above
- Topped by renewable slightly convex surface of small stones and gravel
- Culverts beneath foundations every 91 m, leading to side drainage ditches
- Road builders had a ring to check size of stones
- Supported by Post Office
- Telford constructed 1,408 km of roads in Scottish highlands and eleven major bridges

A McAdam road

- More economical to build
- Road beds dry and firm, well drained
- Successive layers of stone taken from earlier roads and broken into pieces
- No rolling necessary as iron-wheeled traffic and rain compacted roads
- Coach horses worked for seven rather than three years on a macadamed road
- Supported by Board of Agriculture
- With his sons, McAdam built over 3,000 km of roads by 1820

London to Manchester			London to Edinburgh		London to Oxford	
4 days	2 days	25 hours	10 days summer 12 days winter	45½ hours	2 days	6 hours
1754	1784	1830	1750s	1830s	1751	1828

A road Rocket

Telford's most famous road bridge was the Menai Suspension Bridge, built of stone and steel. This joined North Wales to Anglesey on the 170 km Shrewsbury to Holyhead road and made access to Ireland easier.

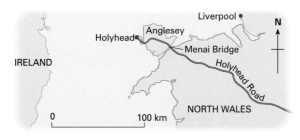

▲ Site of the Menai Bridge

▲ Telford's Menai Bridge, 1826, with a stage-coach crossing from North Wales to Anglesey

New and better roads such as this cut down journey times and increased traffic and travel. By 1820 a thousand coaches left London each morning to all parts of Britain. There were 321 services between the City, Westminster and the suburbs south of the Thames. 2,500 horses were kept at the first western 'change' at Hounslow. Stockbrokers could even commute from Brighton!

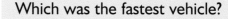

Which was the fastest vehicle?

The mailcoach. Its team of four horses could pull a coach at 10 miles (16 km) per hour non-stop for an hour.

▲ A Devonshire mail coach, 1840, with inn and turnpike

Stages for a change of horse were marked by coaching inns at roughly ten-mile intervals. Milestones, compulsory on turnpiked roads since 1766, marked the routes. Coach travel, with its fares, overnight accommodation and tips, was expensive. The poor walked or went by the much cheaper stage wagon.

In 1836 William Chapman owned 3,000 coaches, 150,000 horses, employed 30,000 drivers, guards and ostlers, and ran twenty-seven mail coaches every night from London. Coach names were evocative – *Lightwing*, *Highflyer*, *Quicksilver* and *Rocket*. The years between 1790 and 1840 have often been called the golden age of the stage coach.

A rail Rocket

The Napoleonic Wars also indirectly helped the development of a new form of transport, the railway.

How?

Horse fodder became expensive, and it was horses that pulled the coal along the wagon-ways. So colliery owners looked again at Trevithick's steam locomotive to see how it could be developed. By 1823 twenty improved locomotives were in use on the coalfields, some designed and driven by a young engineer, George Stephenson.

In 1821 a wealthy landowner, Edward Pease, appointed Stephenson to construct a 43 km railway from Witton Park colliery at Darlington to the port of Stockton-on-Tees.

Pease assumed the carts would be horse-drawn. Stephenson persuaded him to include steam locomotives and built one – Locomotion No. 1 – for the task. At the line's opening in 1825, this engine pulled twelve loaded wagons, a coach and twenty-one passenger cars. In service it continued to pull coal (75 tonnes at 8 km per hour) and passengers. When it reached 12 km per hour going downhill some passengers were terrified!

▲ The opening of the Stockton and Darlington railway, September 23 1825

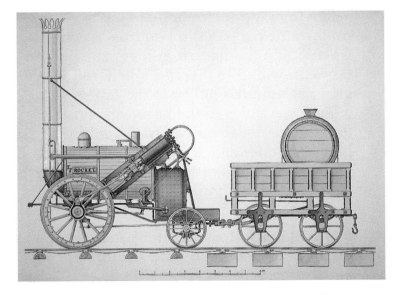

▲ The Rocket

After this success George was appointed Chief Engineer – and his son, Robert, Chief Surveyor – of the Liverpool and Manchester line. At the Rainhill Trials, a competition for the best locomotive to operate the line, the Stephensons' Rocket reached 30 km per hour and won easily against three competitors.

The Liverpool and Manchester line, opened in 1830, was for goods and passengers. In 1831, with over a thousand passengers a day and a large volume of freight, profits leapt to £80,000. This was, indeed, a revolution in land transport.

1830 Liverpool and Manchester railway

The first inter-city line

▲ The Sankey Viaduct, 20 m high

Building the new railways presented huge technical problems. The navvies with their shovels, picks, crowbars and wheelbarrows dug vast quantities of soil, clay and rock by hand to make tunnels, cuttings, embankments and bridges.

The Liverpool and Manchester railway, as illustrated here, had its share of challenges.

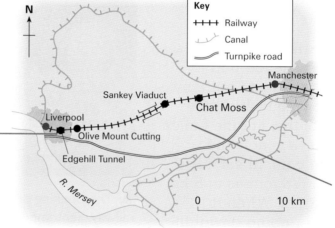

Edgehill tunnel: problems included flooding and roof collapse. The navvies had to bore a tunnel through almost 2 km of solid rock

Brushwood was tipped into peat and quicksand bog to make a raft which floated and formed the foundations for the embankment

▲ Making the running

When 'making the running', planks were laid up the sides of a cutting and the navvy wheeled up the barrow. A rope, attached to the barrow and to the man's belt, ran up the side and round a pulley at the top. When a signal was given to the horse drawer at the top, the man was drawn up the side, balancing the loaded barrow on the plank. If the horse slipped or the man lost his balance, he had to save himself by throwing the barrow to one side and himself to the other.

It is perhaps not surprising that these strong fearless men, after shifting ten tonnes of earth every day, acquired a reputation as big drinkers, eaters and fighters.

Radical: A person who wants to see great changes in political, economic and social affairs	Cobbett: Publishes weekly register on reform	'Orator' Henry Hunt	Francis Place: Tailor	Burdett and Hume: Radical MPs	Hume Bentham Roebuck	Attwood's Political Union for electoral reform

Radicals push for reform

1829 December

The Swing Riots

As railways began to replace coaches, as factory machines replaced hand workers, so farm machines replaced agricultural workers. In the 1820s many farmers had bought threshing-machines which could do several days' threshing in a few hours.

What effect did this have?

Threshing had traditionally been a source of winter work for labourers, so the disappearance of this work in times of general hardship added to their grinding poverty.

1830 produced a poor harvest and the price of bread rose. In the south and south-eastern counties where the Speenhamland system was used most, attempts were made to keep down the poor rates by doling out potatoes and oatmeal rather than money. Farmers refused to raise wages, and some even tried to reduce them. There was no alternative means of employment. On top of this, Church of England clergymen still expected their tithes.

▲ A threshing (thrashing) machine

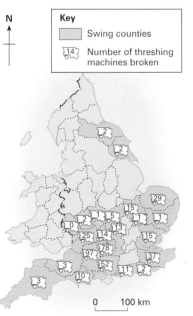

Key

Swing counties

[14] Number of threshing machines broken

0   100 km

▲ Counties where Swing Riots occurred, 1830

The riots which followed in several counties were an expression of the distress felt. The workers wanted higher wages and assurance that the Poor Law rate would be paid. A certain 'Captain Swing' wrote threatening letters to farmers. Harsh overseers of the poor were ducked in village ponds, hay-stacks were set alight and threshing machines smashed.

The Whig government responded with severity. Nine rioters – men and boys – were hanged, and 450 transported, 200 for life. These measures contributed to the growing resentment against the government and fuelled the demand for reform of Parliament.

Death of George III	His sons:	Prince Regent (1811) George IV	Frederick Duke of York (died 1827)	William Duke of Clarence William IV	Edward Duke of Kent Father of Victoria	Ernest Duke of Cumberland	Augustus Duke of Sussex	Adolphus Duke of Cambridge
1820	1820–1830			1830–1837				

George IV, William IV

George IV died in 1830. Monarchy was at its lowest ebb, and because of newspapers and cheap prints which were carried all over the country by the mail coach, more people were aware of the reasons why.

▲ Gillray's cartoon of 1797: 'A voluptuary under the horrors of Digestion'

Cartoons such as this, drawn when George was Prince Regent, commented on a lifestyle devoted to pleasure, chiefly his own.

The future king's stomach is bursting out at his trouser buttons. He is picking his teeth with a fork. A chamberpot acts as a paperweight for his unpaid bills: tradesmen would try to stop him in the street to claim their money! Medicines include cures for piles and stinking breath. Two bottles contain quack remedies for venereal disease. It was quite common for him to drink three bottles of claret before dinner.

George IV was responsible for the design and restoration of some wonderful buildings, but spending £10 million in seven years on the Brighton Pavilion was insensitive at a time of social unrest and distress.

Agitation for parliamentary reform increased, but after the election of 1830, the new Tory Prime Minister, the Duke of Wellington, dismissed the idea. He declared that 'the system of representation possessed the full and entire confidence of the country'. Wellington lost the confidence of Parliament, however, and resigned shortly afterwards. The next Prime Minister, the Whig Lord Grey, was appointed by William IV and accepted the introduction of a Reform Bill as part of his ministry.

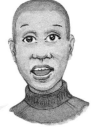

Did the Whigs want reform?

They were aware of public opinion and knew that some change was necessary. But both Whigs and Tories wanted to preserve the traditional constitution and the privileges of the land-owning classes.

'Potwalloper': Every man whose house had a hearth could vote	'Burgage': Vote depended on ownership of certain land	'Corporation': Only members of town council could vote	'Scot and Lot': All male ratepayers could vote	'Rotten': Tiny places with few voters	'Pocket': Controlled by a particular family

1831 Borough franchises varied

Town and county

Who was eligible to vote in parliamentary elections in 1830?

In a county constituency (area) you could vote if you possessed a freehold property valued at forty shillings a year. This right had been granted in 1430!

You could vote in a town constituency if you lived in a town which had the status and special privileges of a borough, granted by royal charter. The last town to be made a borough was Newark, in 1677. This meant that the 'new' towns of the Industrial Revolution, such as Manchester with 182,000 inhabitants, could not be represented in Parliament, and no voting took place there.

Even if you lived in a borough, the franchise (voting rights) depended on local medieval customs. You could vote in Preston as long as you stayed there the night before the election. In about twelve boroughs anyone who boiled a pot ('potwallopers') – that is, all male householders or lodgers – could vote. In nearly forty boroughs, anyone who was a 'burgage tenant' (those owning certain tenements) could vote. In nearly fifty boroughs, anyone who paid 'scot and lot', church and poor rates, could vote.

It seems an illogical franchise!

So was the distribution of seats.

No matter what size the electorate (number of voters) was, both counties and boroughs could return (be represented by) two MPs each. So Yorkshire, with 16,000 voters, and Pontefract, a borough in Yorkshire with 623 voters, both returned two MPs. 'Rotten boroughs', such as Old Sarum, Wiltshire, with seven voters, and Appleby, Cumbria, with one voter, returned two MPs. The 'rotten' (and crumbling!) Dunwich, which was falling into the sea, also returned two MPs.

But not only was the system illogical: it was also open to influence, patronage, bribery and corruption.

▲ Three rotten boroughs

408,000 men in a population of 24 million voted for 558 MPs	400 MPs elected in boroughs	50 boroughs had fewer than 40 voters	No women were allowed to vote	No one under 21 could vote	

1831

Bribery and corruption

How were people influenced as to how they should vote?

The fact that voting was not secret made a difference.

Voters had to stand and announce the name of the candidate they were voting for, and the decision was then recorded in writing. Some voters in boroughs were 'in the pocket' of their local landowners who owned most of the property. They voted for their landowner or his preferred candidate. A voter was unlikely to declare the name of a rival candidate if he had been threatened with eviction or feared loss of work.

▲ Election scene, Covent Garden, London, 1818

Underhand practices, particularly bribery, were common. Voters declared for the candidate who offered the most cash. The 'nabobs' openly bought their way into Parliament. Bribes also took the form of free beer, wine, rabbit or game and promises of jobs.

Elections were regarded as rather like holidays. They afforded much witty comment and amusement; candidates had their own coloured ribbons; there were songs, bands and processions. Innkeepers welcomed the extra money.

Candidates needed to be wealthy, as they had to cover all expenses. These would include leafleting, 'gifts', banquets and the cost of accommodating voters brought in from outside. As elections could last longer than a fortnight, these costs could be considerable.

Corruption was rife. People were sometimes kept drunk for days until voting was closed. The sick and certified insane were brought out to vote. Men were often hired to impersonate voters. Dead men 'voted' several times. Fights and brawls regularly broke out.

Parliamentary reform was long overdue.

▲ The unfit and unwell are brought to vote

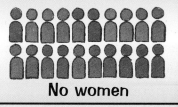
The Reform Bill

The Reform Bill of March 1831 proposed to abolish 168 seats and replace these with 106 seats. The franchise in boroughs was for men who occupied, as owner or tenant, property valued at £10 or over. The franchise in counties was kept by the forty-shilling freeholder and extended to the £10 copyholder and £50 leaseholder.

Was the Bill passed?

The Commons passed it by one vote, but it was defeated at a committee stage.

The following general election was fought for the first time on one issue – this question of reform.

In June 1831, a new Reform Bill was passed by a large majority in the Commons, but it was defeated by the Lords in October. The country protested. Political unions held meetings and demonstrations where the slogan 'The Bill, the whole Bill and nothing but the Bill!' was chanted. Peers and bishops were insulted in the street. Mobs destroyed Nottingham Castle, Derby Gaol and the Bishop's Palace at Bristol.

The government introduced another Reform Bill, with some concessions to win moderate Tories over. This passed the Commons and Lords, but was halted at a committee stage again.

Lord Grey, the Prime Minister, asked William IV to create 50 new peers to secure a government majority. The King refused, so Grey resigned. The King then asked Wellington to take over, but he had insufficient support.

Grey was recalled and the King agreed to create the peers if necessary when the Reform Bill reached the Lords. This time the Tory peers, not wanting to be swamped with Whig peers, passed the Bill. It became law in June, 1832. The country celebrated with bonfires, lighted windows, toasts and speeches.

▲ Reform riots at Bristol, 1831

77

The Great Reform Bill

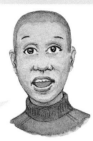

Why was it called 'Great'?

One observer commented that 'it was not a good bill, though it was a great bill when it was passed'.

That the bill had been made law was cause for celebration. The size of the electorate increased from about 400,000 to 900,000 in a population of 24 million. Elections became more organised as voters had to register, polling districts were introduced, and the duration of polls was reduced.

People soon realised, however, that it did not lead to many immediate changes. When the reformed Parliament assembled after a general election in December 1833, it turned out to be very much like any other Parliament. Both sides of the House of Commons were full of country gentlemen, with 217 sons of peers or baronets among them. 115 members still sat for boroughs with fewer than 500 voters. There were few representatives from the new industrial and commercial middle classes.

How many working-class representatives were there?

None. Working men, to qualify for the vote, needed an income of about £150 a year. Few seldom earned more than £50 a year.

Key
Counties gaining two seats
Counties gaining one seat
• New boroughs with two seats
• New boroughs with one seat

▲ Parliamentary reform, 1832

An industrial town such as Leeds did gain two seats, but out of a population of 123,000 only about 5,000 were eligible to vote.

Bitterly disappointed, working men turned to other means to secure a more democratic society.

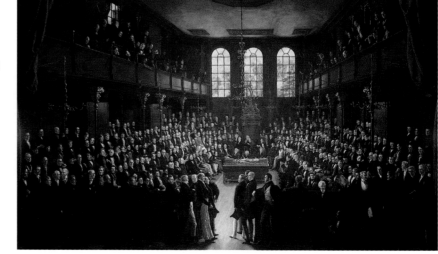

▲ The reformed House of Commons, 1833

Out of population of 18 million in England, 7 million are actively involved in religion	52% Anglican (Church of England)	21% Methodists	20% Other Nonconformists	4% Roman Catholics

1851 Religious census (estimates)

Church and chapel

Why were bishops insulted and a bishop's palace attacked in 1831?

Twenty-one out of twenty-three bishops in the House of Lords had voted against the Reform Bill.

Many felt that the bishops, who enjoyed great wealth, were like their Church, out of touch with ordinary working people. In villages, the influence of the Church remained strong. There, the parson and squire ruled in tandem. Both were usually the chief landowners, and the parson continued to receive tithes from his tenants.

The hierarchy in society was mirrored in the church itself. The rich, in comfortable pews, received holy communion first. The poor, having curtsied to the parson's wife, sat at the back on benches and listened to sermons which preached obedience. 'God made the low and mighty and ordered their estate [place in society]' went the words of one hymn.

In towns the influence of the Church was noticeably less. There was a practical reason for this. Population grew rapidly but no new churches were built to accommodate worshippers. As parishes grew, the parson rarely contacted his new residents.

Parsons appointed poorly paid curates to work on their behalf. Many curates worked tirelessly for their poorest parishioners. The Evangelicals, a middle-class group of Christians, urged the Church to reach out into new industrial cities.

Often several new chapels *were* built in these areas but they belonged to the Dissenting Nonconformists, the Quakers, the Baptists and the Congregationalists, who did strive to reach out to the poor. One group, the Methodists, had an enormous impact on the lives of ordinary working people.

▲ Cartoon of a Church of England clergyman, 1829

Trained as Anglican priest	Worked out a methodical series of prayers and study	This earned him the label 'Methodist'	Preached on hillsides, in fields, from tops of walls	Travelled 200,000 miles on horseback	Preached 40,000 sermons	Powerful emotional speaker

1703–1791 John Wesley

The Methodists

Why did the Methodists have such an impact?

One reason was the personality of their founder, John Wesley.

He had trained as an Anglican priest and in 1738, during a service, he suddenly experienced a deep religious feeling. He wrote, 'I felt my heart strangely warmed.' From that moment he knew that God loved him and that he was 'saved'. He wanted people to let him save them, too, and began to preach a Christian message that the ordinary worker understood.

Wesley felt that everyone, rich or poor, was a sinner. If people stopped swearing, drinking and gambling, and led a Christian life, they would be saved from Hell. When local priests, disliking his message and methods, refused to let him preach from their pulpits, he began to preach outdoors. He rode thousands of miles and took the word of God to Cornish tinners, Durham miners, Staffordshire potters and many others.

▲ Wesley preaching from his father's tomb

In 1784 Wesley reluctantly broke away from the Anglican Church to organise the Methodist Church. Wesley's organisation was efficient and effective. Twelve people formed a 'class' (a discussion group), and met in each other's homes or in barns or warehouses. One of them was elected as a preacher. Several classes could join to build a chapel and appoint a minister.

In these chapels they sang tuneful, joyful hymns, some composed by Wesley's brother Charles, and listened to simple but powerful sermons. They came away with a belief that in the eyes of God they were as good as the next person. They came away determined to change their ways and convert others. By 1815 there were a quarter of a million Methodists in Britain.

'all relief to the able-bodied person or their families other than in regulated workhouses shall be unlawful and shall cease'

'making the workhouse an uninviting place of wholesome restraint'

1834 Report of the Royal Commission

The Poor Law Amendment Act

MORE
16
REFORM

While the Churches tried to help the poor, the government addressed the problem of poverty. It felt that the old system of Poor Law rates, particularly the Speenhamland 'allowance', encouraged the able-bodied poor to be idle and 'live on the parish'. It decided to stop outdoor relief and continue with indoor relief only.

What is indoor relief?

It is when relief in the form of shelter, food and clothing is given in workhouses.

Workhouses had been legal since 1723 and, since an Act of 1783, had become refuges for paupers, the old and the sick. The government proposed to continue relief for the old and sick in their homes but to offer indoor relief to the poor only if they lived in the workhouse. To make sure only the genuine poor applied to enter, conditions inside were deliberately made 'less eligible' – so unattractive, in fact, that only the desperate would want to live there.

Under the Act:

*   Parishes were to combine to form unions; these had to provide workhouses.

*   Each union was governed by a Board of Guardians.

*   Guardians appointed salaried officials – an overseer, a master of the workhouse and a medical officer – to look after the poor.

The unions were governed centrally from London, where three commissioners supervised the work of the Guardians.

By 1847, four-fifths of the 647 Poor Law unions had built new workhouses.

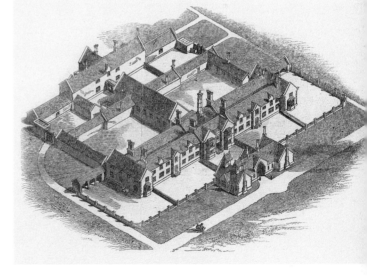

▲ Andover Workhouse, 1847, which served a group of parishes

Was the scheme successful?

It was certainly cost-effective.

Even though population was increasing, expenditure on poor relief, which was £7 million in 1832, fell to £4 million by 1837. There was a price to pay for this cost-effectiveness. This was the cost in terms of human suffering.

Rise Roll call Prayers	Breakfast: meals in silence	Men: bone-crushing for glue and fertiliser, oakum picking	Women: scrubbing, cleaning, preparing food	Children: 3 hours' schooling, including Bible reading	Dinner	Work	Supper Prayers	Bed
6 am	6.30–7 am	7–12 am			12–1 pm	1–6 pm	6–7 pm	8 pm

The workhouse

What distressed the poor was the humiliation and shame they were made to feel on entering the workhouse. No personal possessions were allowed, and trips outside and visitors were strictly limited.

They were given workhouse clothes, with no underwear provided, and re-issued old shoes to wear. Hair was cut short to prevent lice. Families were segregated and parents had no more children. This was a drab, miserable existence – as it was designed to be.

Workhouses sound rather prison-like.

The poor christened them 'Bastilles', after the famous French prison.

Most places did offer adequate, if monotonous, diet and medical care, though isolated incidents of cruelty were reported. At Fareham, bed-wetting infants were placed in the stocks. At Andover the men were so hungry that, instead of crushing the putrid bones of horses to make manure, they gnawed at them.

▲ 'Please sir, may I have some more?' Oliver Twist in the workhouse

There were protests, and attacks in the press. Charles Dickens, the famous novelist, wrote *Oliver Twist*, highlighting the plight of pauper children in the workhouse.

There were riots, particularly in the north. Those who, through no fault of their own, had been thrown out of work, objected to entering a workhouse to avoid starvation.

Outdoor relief was continued in the industrial areas as workhouses could not cope with the thousands of unemployed and their families. And protests from the anti-Poor Law campaigners did succeed in changing legislation to make workhouses generally more humane.

Factory reform

The earlier practice of buying up batches of pauper and orphan children of seven years old from workhouses to work in mines and factories meant that thousands of children worked without anyone to protect them from ill-treatment or over-long hours of work. Families living in poverty were also open to exploitation, as they relied on the money that their children brought home.

In 1830 a series of letters appeared in the *Leeds Mercury* newspaper. The writer, Richard Oastler, who was an Evangelical, compared child labour in the mills of Bradford with negro slavery on the plantations.

Soon a powerful movement grew in support of a ten-hour working day. A Tory Evangelical MP, Michael Sadler, introduced the Ten Hour Bill in Parliament. Supporters of the Bill had given evidence to a Select Committee, but Parliament was reluctant to hear it.

Why?

They tended to side with the employers, who argued that shorter working hours would lead to higher prices for goods and Britain losing trade.

Sadler lost his seat at the next election and the campaign was taken up by Lord Ashley (later Earl of Shaftesbury).

Parliament set up a Commission of Inquiry, as it was suspicious of some evidence offered by the Select Committee. Some reports were discredited, but complaints of bullying, ill-health, injuries and long hours were confirmed in a great number of cases.

The government found that it had to intervene to protect the weakest members of society. Yet the ten-hour day was not immediately achieved. It was many years before this and many necessary reforms took place.

▲ Working a bellows: three pence a day for 15 hours' work

One inspector had 2,142 mills in Yorks. and Lancs. to inspect	Birth registers set up	Possible to check age of 8 year olds	Ten Hour Act followed mass meetings, petitions and processions	Plight of chimney-sweep boys highlighted in Charles Kingsley's 'The Water Babies'
1833	1836	1844	1847	1863

Factory legislation

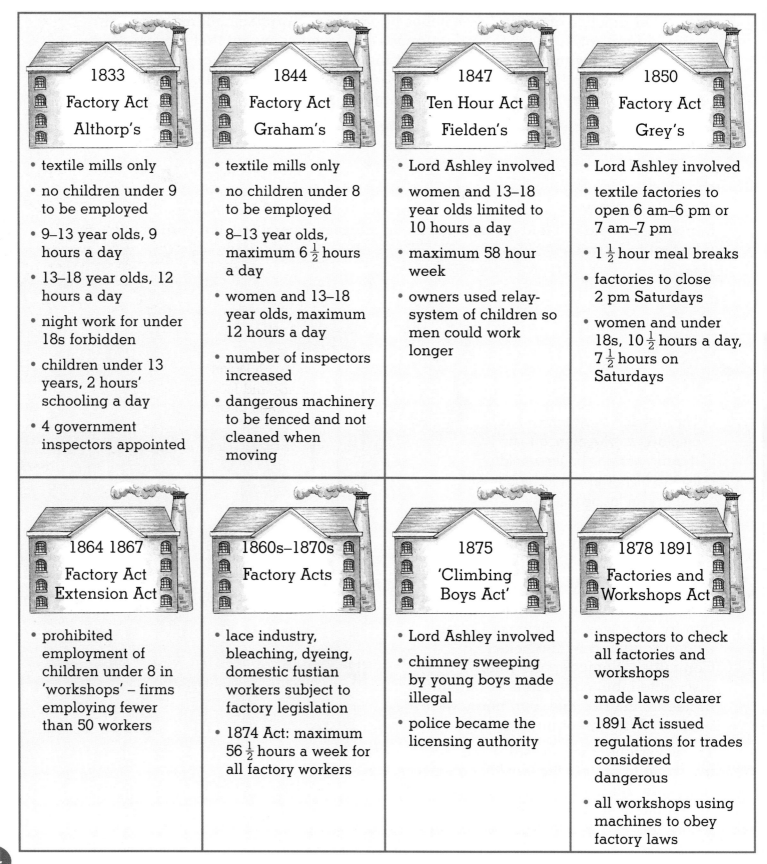

1833

Factory Act

Althorp's

- textile mills only
- no children under 9 to be employed
- 9–13 year olds, 9 hours a day
- 13–18 year olds, 12 hours a day
- night work for under 18s forbidden
- children under 13 years, 2 hours' schooling a day
- 4 government inspectors appointed

1844

Factory Act

Graham's

- textile mills only
- no children under 8 to be employed
- 8–13 year olds, maximum $6\frac{1}{2}$ hours a day
- women and 13–18 year olds, maximum 12 hours a day
- number of inspectors increased
- dangerous machinery to be fenced and not cleaned when moving

1847

Ten Hour Act

Fielden's

- Lord Ashley involved
- women and 13–18 year olds limited to 10 hours a day
- maximum 58 hour week
- owners used relay-system of children so men could work longer

1850

Factory Act

Grey's

- Lord Ashley involved
- textile factories to open 6 am–6 pm or 7 am–7 pm
- $1\frac{1}{2}$ hour meal breaks
- factories to close 2 pm Saturdays
- women and under 18s, $10\frac{1}{2}$ hours a day, $7\frac{1}{2}$ hours on Saturdays

1864 1867

Factory Act Extension Act

- prohibited employment of children under 8 in 'workshops' – firms employing fewer than 50 workers

1860s–1870s

Factory Acts

- lace industry, bleaching, dyeing, domestic fustian workers subject to factory legislation
- 1874 Act: maximum $56\frac{1}{2}$ hours a week for all factory workers

1875

'Climbing Boys Act'

- Lord Ashley involved
- chimney sweeping by young boys made illegal
- police became the licensing authority

1878 1891

Factories and Workshops Act

- inspectors to check all factories and workshops
- made laws clearer
- 1891 Act issued regulations for trades considered dangerous
- all workshops using machines to obey factory laws

Cause	Explosion	Suffocation by gases	Flooding from old workings	Falling of earth	Chains, ropes breaking	Run over by wagons	Boilers bursting
No. of accidents	87	4	4	15	19	13	5
Deaths	1,243	18	83	33	45	12	34

1799–1840 Northumberland and Durham coalfields

Conditions in mines

This diagram of a mine shows how deep child-trappers had to work. Trappers helped ventilate the mine. As air entered, it was split and, by using trap-doors, was sent to different coal faces and workings. By 1830 mines could be 150 metres deep.

Ventilation was only one of the many problems facing miners in their dangerous occupation.

The Davy lamp: ▶
its flame was shielded
from explosive gases
by copper gauze

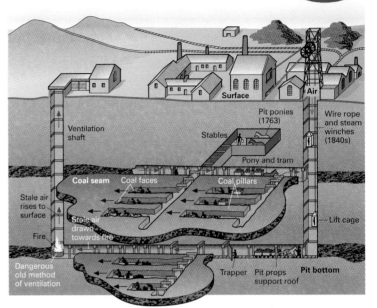

▲ Cross-section of a mine

Problems	Year	Some Solutions
Gases		Wafted air away with jacket
Choke damp (carbon dioxide): miners choked		Brought to surface and face pushed into hole in ground to force lungs to cough out gas
After damp (carbon monoxide): poisonous		Canaries
Fire damp (methane): explosive		Candles on long sticks held by 'firemen'
		Candles on backs of pit ponies
	1815	Davy lamp: flame turned blue if gas present
Flooding	1711	Newcomen's steam pump
	1790s	Watt's steam pump
	1850s	Most steam pumps at bottom of shaft
Roof collapse		Pillars of coal, then wooden pit props, to support roof
Ventilation		Wire basket of burning coals to draw stale air out
		Air entering mine split, then channelled by trap-doors
	1807	First mechanical ventilator to pump stale air out
Hauling		Wicker baskets (corves)
		Ponies and trams: wooden wheels and tracks
		Iron wheels
	1767	Iron rails
	1850	Compressed air to pull tubs
Winding		Windlass to pull ropes and buckets
		Cog and gin; whim gin
		Invention of wire ropes
Coal dust: caused silicosis of lungs	1829	No solution

Mine reform

Lord Ashley also headed a Commission which enquired into working conditions in coal mines.

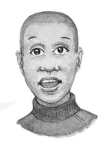

What did he want to do?

He and others wanted to ban the employment of women and children underground.

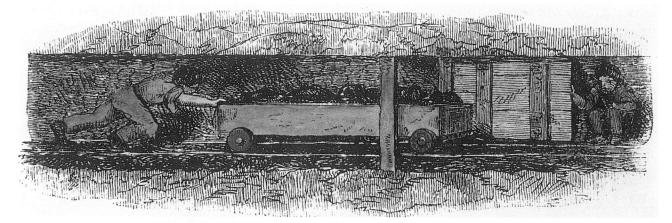

▲ Trappers as young as five worked twelve hours a day

▲ Women and girls aged six to sixty carried heavy loads up ladders, ten hours a day

In 1842 he introduced his Coal Mining Bill to the Commons. He spoke of the blackness of the mines. He told of children of five or six who crawled through traps no more than 60 cm high, pushing the smaller coal carriages.

He described others required to lie on their backs in the damp, foul atmosphere, opening and shutting air-vents by means of strings attached to their hands and feet. Some, he said, stood barefoot in pools of water for periods of up to twelve hours working the shaft-pumps.

He compared the older boys and girls and women to pit ponies as they were made to crawl on hands and feet, drawing full-size coal-trucks along narrow tunnels.

He drew attention to the sufferings of pauper children from workhouse orphanages who, from the age of seven, could be made to work eighty or ninety hours a week with no one to protect them. MPs were even more shocked to hear that children of both sexes worked almost naked in the presence of naked adults.

Lord Ashley spoke for two hours. He asked, 'Where is the right to inflict a servitude like this? Undo the heavy burden and let the oppressed go free.' At the end of his address, many MPs were so overcome with emotion they left the chamber to recover their composure. By the end of July 1842, the Bill was made law.

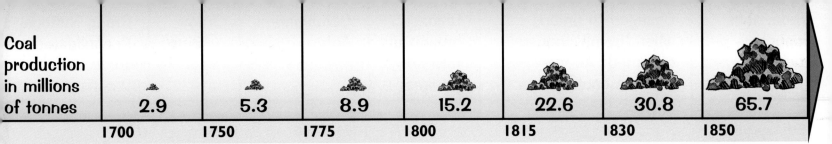

Coal production in millions of tonnes	2.9	5.3	8.9	15.2	22.6	30.8	65.7
	1700	1750	1775	1800	1815	1830	1850

Coal, steam and iron

Was the production of coal important to the economy?

It was vital. Coal underpinned the Industrial Revolution. It was the fuel that drove the wheels of industrial progress.

Coal, steam and iron were inextricably linked. When these three were harnessed to the invention of the railway, the wheels of progress accelerated rapidly.

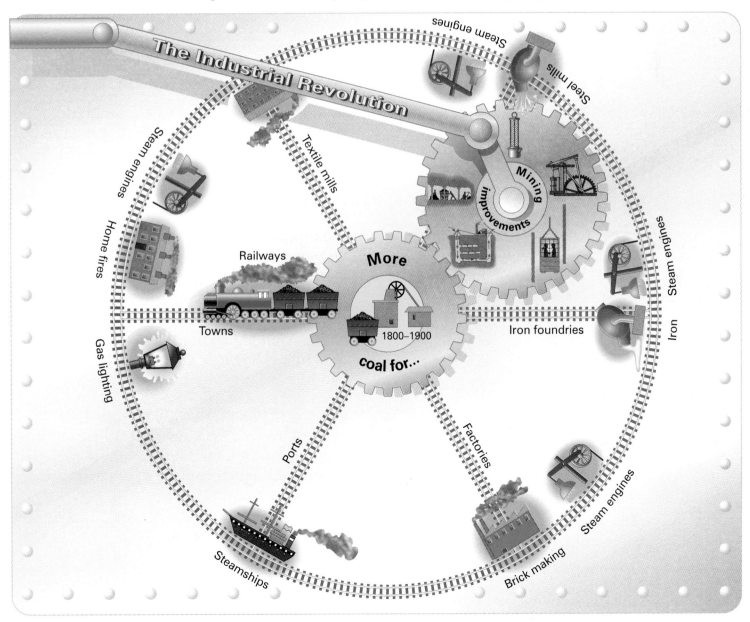

Yet mining remained hard manual labour with a pick and shovel. One miner in every two hundred died at work in the pits.

Trade clubs Friendly societies	Changed to unions when 'tramp' money collected: workers could tramp to another place for work	Unions organised turnouts (strikes)	Combination Acts	Trade unions legal	Grand National Consolidated Trade Union
18th century			1799–1800	1825	1834

Early trade unions

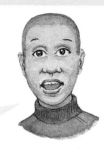

Didn't miners have a trade union to work on their behalf for better working conditions?

Trade unions were not legal until 1825.

During the French Revolutionary wars, the government, fearing that workers might use unions as cover for anti-government political activities, banned meetings under the Combination Acts of 1799 and 1800. Workers were forbidden to 'combine' – to meet so that they could plan joint action to raise wages or shorten working hours, either by bargaining with or threatening their employers. Most unions continued to meet in secret, and prosecutions were few.

In 1824, when government fears had subsided and the economy had generally improved, the Combination Acts were repealed. So many strikes and wage demands followed, however, that the Acts were amended.

▲ Trade union membership card, 1833

In 1825 trade unions were made legal, but workers could not obstruct or molest an employer or worker during a strike or at any other time. Despite this restriction, unions were formed, and the trade union movement came under the influence of Robert Owen, the factory owner and reformer.

Owen, well known for his work in providing housing, schools and good working conditions for his employees, had tried other social experiments such as model villages. Although these had failed, he was still keen to change society. He thought that if unions were joined into a simple national movement, they could do much to improve working-class conditions.

In January 1834 he persuaded a number of unions to form a Grand National Consolidated Trade Union (GNCTU). He wanted workers in each industry to set up their own workshops and exchange each other's products through a co-operative organisation. The GNCTU, which was soon successful, attracted 500,000 members.

The Tolpuddle Martyrs

> Did this high membership of the GNCTU alarm employers?

> It certainly did. They feared that workers might take over their businesses and take control of the whole industry itself.

CAUTION.

WHEREAS it has been represented to us from several quarters, that mischievous and designing Persons have been for some time past, endeavouring to induce, and have induced, many Labourers in various Parishes in this County, to attend Meetings, and to enter into Illegal Societies or Unions, to which they bind themselves by unlawful oaths, administered secretly by Persons concealed, who artfully deceive the ignorant and unwary,—WE, the undersigned Justices think it our duty to give this PUBLIC NOTICE and CAUTION, that all Persons may know the danger they incur by entering into such Societies.

ANY PERSON who shall become a Member of such a Society, or take any Oath, or assent to any Test or Declaration not authorized by Law—

Any Person who shall administer, or be present at, or consenting to the administering or taking any Unlawful Oath, or who shall cause such Oath to be administered, although not actually present at the time—

Any Person who shall not reveal or discover any Illegal Oath which may have been administered, or any Illegal Act done or to be done—

Any Person who shall induce, or endeavour to persuade any other Person to become a Member of such Societies,

WILL BECOME

Guilty of Felony,

AND BE LIABLE TO BE

Transported for Seven Years.

ANY PERSON who shall be compelled to take such an Oath, unless he shall declare the same within four days, together with the whole of what he shall know touching the same, will be liable to the same Penalty.

Any Person who shall directly or indirectly maintain correspondence or intercourse with such Society, will be deemed Guilty of an Unlawful Combination and Confederacy, and on Conviction before one Justice, on the Oath of one Witness, be liable to a Penalty of TWENTY POUNDS, or to be committed to the Common Gaol or House of Correction, for THREE CALENDAR MONTHS; or if proceeded against by Indictment, may be CONVICTED OF FELONY, and be TRANSPORTED FOR SEVEN YEARS.

Any Person knowingly permit any Meeting of any such Society to be held in any House, Building, or other Place, shall for the first offence be liable to the Penalty of FIVE POUNDS; and for every other offence committed after Conviction, be deemed Guilty of such Unlawful Combination and Confederacy, and on Conviction before one Justice, on the Oath of one Witness, be liable to a Penalty of TWENTY POUNDS, or to be committed to the Common Gaol or House of Correction, FOR THREE CALENDAR MONTHS; or if proceeded against by Indictment may be

CONVICTED OF FELONY,

And Transported for SEVEN YEARS.

COUNTY OF DORSET.　　C. B. WOLLASTON,　　HENRY FRAMPTON,
Dorchester Division.　　JAMES FRAMPTON,　　RICHD. TUCKER STEWARD,
　　　　　WILLIAM ENGLAND,　　WILLIAM R. CHURCHILL,
February 22d, 1834.　　THOS. DADE,　　AUGUSTUS FOSTER.
　　　　　JNO. MORTON COLSON.

G. CLARK, PRINTER, CORNHILL, DORCHESTER.

▲ The Dorset magistrates' notice

Employers urged the government to take action against the unions. An opportunity came in March 1834. A group of farm workers in Tolpuddle, Dorset, whose wages had been reduced, wanted to join the GNCTU by setting up a Society of Agricultural Labourers.

In common with other societies, the leader, George Loveless, a local Methodist lay preacher, decided on a secret initiation ceremony. This involved kissing the Bible and swearing an oath. Although prosecutions were rare, this was in fact illegal under an Act of 1797. Hearing of the ceremony, Dorset magistrates printed and circulated a warning notice.

One week later the Tolpuddle men were arrested on a charge of administering an unlawful oath. The sentence for Loveless and five others was transportation to Australia for seven years. There was a public outcry. Meetings and demonstrations were held and petitions signed.

It was not until 1836 that a royal pardon was granted; the men were brought back in 1838 and 1839. In the short term the sentence had its desired effect. By the end of 1835 the GNCTU was dissolved. Many employers presented workers with 'the document': men had to sign a promise not to join a union or be dismissed.

The attempt to achieve better working conditions through unions seemed to have failed.

▲ 30,000 attend a rally led by Robert Owen

| Votes for men over 21 | Secret ballot | No property qualifications for MPs | Payment for MPs | Equal constituencies | Annual elections |

1838 Six aims of the Charter

The Chartist movement

One organiser of the petitions for the release of the Tolpuddle Martyrs was William Lovett, a skilled cabinet-maker. He and Francis Place, a master tailor who had helped to bring about the repeal of the Combination Acts, belonged to the London Working Men's Association, which was set up in 1836.

These two and many others turned away from union activity to work again for Parliamentary reform. They wanted working men as MPs in Parliament. Only then, they thought, would laws be passed to help improve the lives and working conditions of ordinary people. In 1838 the association issued a charter.

1. If every man had the vote then MPs would have to take into account how those men voted.

3. Working people who did not own land could stand for Parliament.

5. All voting districts to have the same number of voters.

The Six Points
OF THE
PEOPLE'S CHARTER

1. A VOTE for every man twenty-one years of age, of sound mind, and not undergoing punishment for crime.

2. THE BALLOT – To protect the elector in the exercise of his vote.

3. NO PROPERTY QUALIFICATION for Members of Parliament – this enabling the constituencies to return the man of their choice, be he rich or poor.

4. PAYMENT OF MEMBERS, thus enabling an honest tradesman, working man, or other person to serve a constituency, when taken from his business to attend to the interests of the country.

5. EQUAL CONSTITUENCIES, securing the same amount of representation for the same number of electors, instead of allowing small constituencies to swamp the vote of large ones.

6. ANNUAL PARLIAMENTS, thus presenting the most effectual check to bribery and intimidation, since though a constituency might be bought once in seven years (even with the ballot), no purse could buy a constituency (under a system of universal suffrage) in each ensuing twelvemonth, and since members, when elected for a year only, would not be able to defy and betray their constituents as now.

2. Secret voting, so employers could not influence how workers voted.

4. MPs to be paid. This would help working men to take a seat in the Commons.

6. This would force MPs to keep in close touch with the voters' wishes.

▲ Handbill of 1838

Was there much support for this movement?

There was, particularly when unemployment was high and bread expensive.

In 1838, a third consecutive poor harvest meant that wheat cost 64% more than in 1835. People supported the Chartists because they were hungry, out of work or on 'short time'. Many supported the movement because they had gained nothing from the Reform Bill of 1832 and because they resented the Poor Law of 1834. Thousands attended rallies in Glasgow, Birmingham and Leeds.

London Working Men's Association	Charter issued	Unemployment and distress: much support for Chartist movement	First petition	Rise of Feargus O'Connor. His newspaper, the Northern Star, achieves a circulation of 50,000 per week	Unemployment and distress: support revives	Second petition
1836	1838		1839	1840s	1841–1842	1842

The first petition

This petition, with 1.3 million signatures, was presented to Parliament in May 1839.

Was it accepted?

The motion even to consider the petition was rejected by 235 votes to 40.

▲ Mayhem in the Commons

The cartoon here demonstrates what many people believed Parliament would look like if the Charter became law. MPs, most of whom were still from the wealthy, landowning classes, did not want changes and greater democracy.

There was little violence when the petition was rejected, apart from in South Wales. Here about 5,000 miners and ironworkers, most armed with sticks and a few with guns, attacked a hotel in Newport to release local Chartist leaders who were held there. The authorities, interpreting the attack as an armed rising, used troops to drive them back, leaving over twenty dead. The leader, the draper John Frost, and two others were transported to Australia for life.

This incident highlighted the differences in leadership within the movement. Some, such as Lovett and Place, favoured winning the support of public opinion and Parliament by peaceful means – petitions, processions and demonstrations. This branch of the movement became known as the 'moral force'.

Others, such as Feargus O'Connor, favoured the use of a general strike or even an armed rising leading to a revolution. This branch of the movement became known as the 'physical force'. Squabbling between the 'forces' at their public meetings (called conventions), the failure of the petition, the rising in Newport and the arrest of leaders all led to a loss of support.

In 1842, when there was another depression in trade and employment, support revived. A second petition was prepared by O'Connor.

▲ Attack on the Westgate Hotel, Newport

The second petition

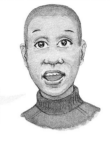

Did Parliament accept this one?

This too was refused a hearing by 287 votes to 49.

▲ The second petition being carried in a procession, 1842

The disturbances which followed were more serious than before and spread from North Staffordshire to the industrial North and Scotland. There were many strikes and riots, and a 'Plug Plot' where stoppers were removed from steam boilers so that the fires that fuelled the mills were extinguished.

The government responded with firm action. Troops put down disorders and hundreds were arrested. As trade revived, support dwindled again.

Most 'moral force' Chartists abandoned the movement. 'Muskets are not what are wanted but education and schooling of the working people,' said Lovett.

O'Connor, who by force of personality had been leader since 1839, now changed tactics. In 1845 he established a scheme similar to that tried by Owen – a co-operative community. He set up the Chartist Co-operative Land Society to help unemployed factory workers move to the countryside. Subscriptions were raised and five estates, one called O'Connorville, were set up.

▲ O'Connorville – an illustration in the *Northern Star*

Unlike Owen's ideal in which everything was owned in common, each of the 500 families cultivated its own plot of land bought on weekly subscription. The society failed to make a profit, however, and ended in 1851.

The years 1847 to 1848 were a time of depression and rising food prices. Support for the Chartists revived and O'Connor planned a third petition.

Votes for men over 21	Secret ballot	No property qualifications for MPs	Payment for MPs	Equal constituencies	Annual elections
1918	1872	1858	1911	1885	1833 1834 1835 not achieved

The aims of the Charter achieved

The third petition

The third petition claimed to contain 5.7 million signatures. A huge rally of Chartists was planned for April 10 1848. Half a million were expected at Kennington Common, South London, and a procession carrying the petition to Parliament was to take place after the meeting. The government saw this as a potentially threatening, even revolutionary, situation. Queen Victoria was moved to safety; 150,000 special constables were enlisted; troops and guns were brought into London; and the aged Duke of Wellington was put in charge of the defence of London.

▲ The meeting on Kennington Common

On the day it rained heavily and only 20,000 Chartists turned up. The crowd found the bridge over the Thames barred by soldiers with artillery and dispersed quietly. The petition had to be taken by three cabs to Parliament. On inspection, it was found to contain fewer than two million signatures, including forged ones such as Victoria Rex, several Dukes of Wellington, April First, No Cheese and Flat Nose!

The movement, discredited by this fiasco, ended in 1850.

Was it a complete failure?

Not in the long term.

Despite internal squabbles and the unfortunate ending, it did give the working classes a sense of solidarity and purpose. This had been the first nationwide movement of working-class protest, and many had become more politically educated.

Chartists did not lose hope but moved into other areas such as trade unions, newspapers and co-operative societies. By 1918, five of the Charter's aims had been absorbed into the parliamentary system.

▲ Cartoon of the Kennington Common meeting. The Duke of Wellington is shown nine times

28 weavers set up retail shop in Toad Lane, Rochdale	74 members: profits £22	130 similar societies: 15,000 members	Co-operative Wholesale Society Manchester (CWS)	546,000 members	Over 3 million members
1844	1845	1851	1863	1881	1914

Co-operatives

Six Chartists and six Owenites were among twenty-eight weavers who set up an extremely successful grocery retail shop in Rochdale in 1844. Each man contributed £1 to the business, called the Rochdale Pioneers' Society. With this money, they bought everyday items such as sugar, oatmeal and candles. They opened the store in the evenings and sold goods at fair prices.

▲ Some of the 'Rochdale Pioneers', photographed in 1860

What was so different between this and other shops?

The idea behind it was very democratic. The profits, instead of going to the twenty-eight weavers, were shared out among the customers in the form of a dividend – according to how many items they had purchased.

Shoppers, because they received their dividends promptly, received immediate personal benefits. Alternatively, they could decide to leave their dividends in, thus ploughing money back into the business and helping it to expand.

These accumulated as shares, on which interest was paid, so members were encouraged to build up savings. Money from profits was set aside for a schoolroom above the shop and a library. Later, profits were used for adult education and other services for members.

In 1863 a Co-operative Wholesale Society (CWS) was set up to buy from producers in large quantities (wholesale) and supply individual stores. In 1875 the CWS manufactured its own products such as biscuits and shoes, using its own flour mills and factories. The co-operative idea was so successful that by 1914 there were three million branches.

▲ Reconstruction of the first Toad Lane store, Rochdale

The 'Penny Black': World's first pre-paid gummed postage stamp	Used to send Anti-Corn Law pamphlet to every voter in England	'At the next election you will have to choose between a bread-taxer and a candidate who will untax the poor.'

1840 May 6   **1842**

The Anti-Corn Law League

THE IRISH **19** FAMINE

During the 1830s merchants and mill-owners had repeatedly demanded that the Corn Laws of 1815 should be repealed (cancelled). If they were, they argued, the price of bread would fall, workers' wages could be reduced, British goods would become cheaper and trade would increase.

In October 1838 a group of businessmen set up the Manchester Association for the Repeal of the Corn Laws. Two leaders were John Bright, a Rochdale factory owner, and Richard Cobden, owner of a local cotton-printing works.

▲ Membership card of the Anti-Corn Law League

Despite holding a large meeting in London, when speakers from all over the country hoped to persuade MPs to repeal the Corn Laws, no action followed. The Manchester group decided to set up a national Anti-Corn Law League. They petitioned, held lectures and meetings, and sent out weekly pamphlets. They hoped to elect eight of their own MPs, including Cobden, to the Commons. Cobden declared, 'We want free trade in corn because we think it is just.'

What is free trade?

Trade without government interference.

The idea was made popular in an influential book, *The Wealth of Nations*, written in 1776 by Adam Smith. He and others believed that goods should be sold at whatever price people were prepared to pay. Governments should not impose customs duties and other restrictions on imports.

Robert Peel, leader of the Conservatives (who were in power), had secretly decided to repeal the Corn Laws, and in 1842 he made duties on corn lower. He held back from repealing the laws, knowing that many Conservatives would resist changes. It was a catastrophe in Ireland, however, that made him change his mind.

Population estimates in Ireland	$2\frac{1}{2}$ million	4 million	5 million	$6\frac{3}{4}$ million	$8\frac{1}{4}$ million	$8\frac{1}{2}$ million	$6\frac{1}{4}$ million	A quarter of population lost through death and emigration
	1767	1781	1800	1821	1841	1845	1850	1851

The Potato Famine

It was reported in the summer of 1845 that a potato blight of 'unusual character' was wiping out crops on the Isle of Wight. By September it had spread to Wexford in Ireland. For about three million Irish labourers, out of a population of eight million, the potato was their staple diet.

What was unusual about the blight?

It was unusual because the infected potatoes, when harvested, looked wholesome.

▲ Starving children searching for potatoes, 1848

Two days later, the tubers had disintegrated into a black putrefying matter. Some of the crops that year had already been lifted, but the blight affected crops over half of Ireland. Many peasants fled their rented cottages and hovels in search of food.

Even before the famine, when even a blanket was considered a luxury, life had been a pitiful struggle. This time the misery grew worse. The crop of 1846 failed completely. The winter of 1846/7 was the longest and coldest in living memory.

Families ate the blight-free *seed* potatoes, so planted fewer for the harvest of 1847. Crops were not completely ruined that year, but starvation was worse.

In 1848 the crop failed completely. The Irish labourers suffered not just in hundreds, but thousands. By the end of 1848, nearly a million people had died – of starvation, of typhus and relapsing fever, of famine dropsy, dysentery and scurvy.

One observer wrote: 'Families, when all was eaten and had no hope left, took their last look at the sun, built up their cottage doors that none might see them die nor hear the groans, and were found weeks afterwards, skeletons on their own hearths.'

Emigration

Peel was determined to repeal the Corn Laws so that grain could be sold to the Irish poor at prices they could afford.

Was he successful?

He was, but on the same day as the repeal in June 1846, he was defeated in Parliament on another issue and resigned.

Before his defeat he had ordered Indian corn and meal to be bought and handed out to the starving Irish. He initiated public work schemes so that poor labourers could earn money.

Ministers from the new Whig government were not so supportive. Charles Trevelyan, a chief civil servant, complained that the Irish exaggerated their misfortune.

Assistance in Ireland was limited to public works programmes funded by the rates. The schemes could not cope with the numbers requiring them, so were abandoned in favour of indoor relief, soup kitchens and workhouses. In 1848 nearly a million people spent time in workhouses built to accommodate 250,000. The demand for relief from distress was still so great that outdoor relief had to be continued. Landlords who could not afford the poor rates cleared tenants off their lands.

Through evictions and hunger, thousands more were forced to leave their homes. Many were helped by voluntary workers. The Quakers set up soup kitchens, the Guinness brewing family provided food and work, the British Relief Association gave funds, and the New York Irish Relief Fund sent nearly £250,000.

Why did America help?

Because by 1848 a million Irish had emigrated, chiefly to America.

▲ Starving peasants demanding to get *into* the workhouse

According to one historian, the million who had emigrated and the million who had died helped to 'solve' the huge unemployment problem that existed in Ireland.

The Fenians

More than a fifth of Irish emigrants who crowded on board often decrepit and overladen 'coffin' ships died before reaching their destination. Few took possessions with them, but what many did carry was a festering and abiding hatred of the British government. On arrival in Europe, Australia or America, they would tell stories of heartless indifference, of evictions and of cartloads of grain and farm produce being taken to Irish ports for export while families died of starvation by the roadside.

▲ Emigrants leaving Ireland

These stories were passed down from generation to generation. Some of the hatred and resentment was channelled into raising men, money and supplies for a new movement, one that wanted an immediate overthrow of British power in Ireland. Their leader, John O'Mahoney, named the group the Fenian Brotherhood, after the Fianna Warriors who had followed a legendary Gaelic hero, Fion Mac Camhail. Thousands in America and Ireland joined the Fenians.

What did the Fenians do?

Fenians in England planned to storm Chester army barracks and send captured arms over to Ireland for a rising. This plot was foiled by an informer.

Other actions included ambushing a closed police cart in Manchester in order to rescue an arrested Fenian. During the attack, a police sergeant was killed. Four Fenians were tried and condemned on questionable evidence.

Their defiance in the face of death and their devotion to the cause earned them the name Manchester Martyrs. Another rescue attempt of fellow Fenians at Clerkenwell resulted in twelve Londoners dead and thirty injured. The British public were outraged, and special constables were recruited in many cities. Tension between Britain and Ireland continued.

In 1873 the Fenians were organised into the Irish Republican Brotherhood.

William Symington: Ran steamer along Forth–Clyde canal	Charlotte Dundas	Bell's Comet: Glasgow to Greenock, displaced 4 coaches	Savannah, partly steam-powered, crosses Atlantic	188 paddle steamers in use, chiefly tugs and estuary ferries	1,400 coastal steamboat services
1798	1802	1813	1819	1821	1840s

'Smokeboats'

FULL STEAM
20
AHEAD

Early emigrants from Ireland sailed in sailing ships, but as steam overtook sail, travel became swifter, safer and more comfortable. Early experiments in steamships took place on canals and rivers.

In 1802 William Symington built the *Charlotte Dundas* for the Forth–Clyde canal. Its James Watt double-acting engine drove a stern paddle-wheel and pulled two heavily laden barges for 30 km.

In 1807 Robert Fulton, an American, designed the first sea-going steamship, the *Clermont*, with Boulton and Watt engines which used a great deal of fuel. Early steamships were seen as helping sail, not replacing it.

▲ The *Charlotte Dundas*

Were they built of wood or iron?

Wood, then wood and iron (known as 'composite-built') and then iron.

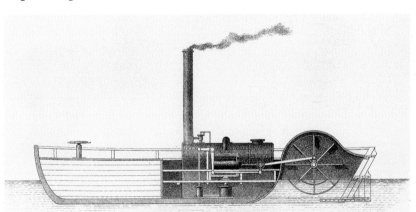

▲ Section drawing of the *Charlotte Dundas*

The ironmaster John Wilkinson had built the first iron vessel, *The Trial*, in 1787. This canal barge had an iron frame and plates, and wooden beams, stern and sternposts.

Iron ships were lighter than wooden ones, displaced less water and carried more cargo. More goods carried meant more profits for the owners.

But it was not only men who preferred iron ships – so did barnacles and weeds. Iron hulls attracted these more quickly than wooden ones, and the balance of ships could become upset. Sometimes the hulls were covered with wooden plates and then copper, but it was found that copper rotted the iron.

This is how the Industrial Revolution developed: by trial and error, problems and solutions. Early ocean-going steamships presented problems. The first to cross the Atlantic, the *Savannah*, could use her engine for only eighty hours during the twenty-day voyage.

Sirius: 700 tonnes, first steam-powered ship to cross Atlantic (18 days)	Great Western: 1,500 tonnes, crosses Atlantic (14 days)	Screw propeller invented	Great Britain: 3,400 tonnes, made of iron, with screw propeller	American clipper James Baines crosses Atlantic (12 days)	Great Eastern: 20,000 tonnes, owners go bankrupt
1838	1838	1838	1845	1854	1858

Sail versus steam

The problem with early steamships was the amount of coal they used. Owners lost money if there was little space for cargo and passengers. The first vessel to cross the Atlantic by steam power alone was the *Sirius*, which left Cork, Ireland, on April 4 1838, taking eighteen days to reach New York. A rival ship, the *Great Western*, also a paddle steamer, left Bristol on April 8 and took fourteen days to reach New York.

The engineer Isambard Kingdom Brunel aimed to link this route with his London to Bristol railway (then under construction) to provide a land–sea route from London to New York. Brunel went on to design the *Great Britain*, which was the first ship to cross the Atlantic powered by a screw propeller: it was also the first to be built entirely of iron.

Brunel's third ship, the *Great Eastern*, the biggest ship of its time, fared less well. On her maiden voyage, a boiler exploded and five people were killed.

Furthermore, steamships could still be out-distanced by clippers.

What were clippers?

The fastest sailing ships ever, reaching a top speed of 16 knots. They were called clippers because they 'clipped' sailing times. They could do the journey from Australia to Britain in sixty days.

Clippers were commercial ships carrying tea from China, wool and grain from Australia and nitrate fertiliser from Chile. The most successful were the composite ships with iron frames and wooden planks. They used steam winches to control a huge amount of sail which gave them their speed.

▲ Brunel's *Great Eastern*, 1858

▲ The *Cutty Sark*, a famous clipper

Steam vessels belonging to United Kingdom	1 vessel: 69 tonnes of shipping	34 vessels: 3,018 tonnes	151 vessels: 15,764 tonnes	295 vessels: 30,009 tonnes	497 vessels: 52,767 tonnes	768 vessels: 87,539 tonnes	912 vessels: 118,140 tonnes	1,142 vessels: 158,729 tonnes
	1814	1820	1825	1830	1835	1840	1845	1849

The decline of sail

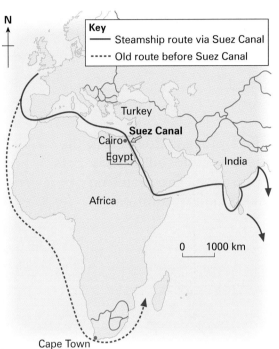

Key
— Steamship route via Suez Canal
---- Old route before Suez Canal

Turkey
Suez Canal
Cairo
Egypt
India
Africa
0   1000 km
Cape Town

▲ The effect of the Suez Canal, 1869

Several factors led to the decline of sailing ships. Clippers were expensive to maintain. Their sails – which could cover fifteen tennis courts – needed 6,500 square metres of canvas and vast amounts of rigging. Then there was a huge crew divided into three watches to man the ship day and night. Also, as sailing ships had to 'tack' from side to side, they were no use on canals.

The Suez Canal, opened in 1869 to link the Mediterranean with the Red Sea, became an important route for steamships, and shortened the passage to India.

When did steam take over from sail?

Though sail continued to be used well into the twentieth century, after 1869 more steamships than sailing ships were built.

Steamships did not have to wait for tides and favourable winds before sailing. Their timetables could state accurate times for delivery of goods and passengers.

Several inventions, including the screw propeller, led to the inevitable decline of sail. One important invention, the compound engine of 1804, was developed in 1854 by John Elder. This re-used the steam from the main cylinder to drive a second piston, so saving coal. Ships could be lighter, carry more cargo and go further. Steel, too, which became cheaper after 1860, made ships lighter.

The British shipbuilding industry thrived. By 1870 more than half the world's tonnage of ships was British. By 1880 the Tyne, with its natural advantages of coal and iron, was the greatest shipbuilding centre in the world.

▲ Out with the old, in with the new: J.M.W. Turner's 1839 painting of the *Fighting Téméraire* (veteran of Trafalgar) being tugged to her last berth to be broken up

Britain produced		$\frac{2}{3}$ world's coal	$\frac{1}{2}$ world's iron	$\frac{5}{7}$ world's steel	$\frac{1}{2}$ world's cotton goods	$\frac{2}{5}$ world's hardware

By 1850

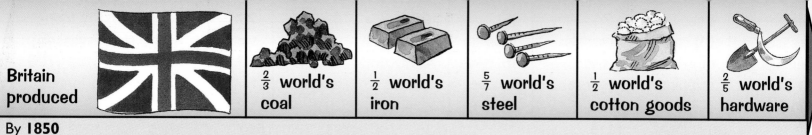

Cheaper steel

How did steel become cheaper?

In 1856 Sir Henry Bessemer produced a converter which turned large quantities of molten iron into steel in just twenty minutes.

Before this, steel production had used Benjamin Huntsmen's process devised in the 1740s. Pieces of blister steel with added charcoal were placed in closed fireclay pots (crucibles) and impurities were burned off in a coke-fired furnace. The resulting steel was of high quality, but as it took three hours to make small quantities, production was costly.

How the Bessemer converter worked

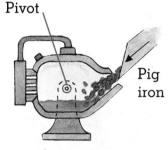

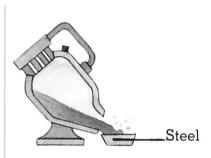

1 Charging (filling) the converter

In Bessemer's process, the molten pig iron was poured straight from the blast furnace into a converter shaped rather like a giant concrete mixer. This could be tilted for filling and emptying.

2 Hot air blast

The converter was turned upright and a blast of hot air was forced through holes in the base. The impurities in the liquid iron were violently expelled in a volcanic surge of white flames and a cascade of sparks.

3 Discharging (emptying) the slag or waste

The slag was poured off.

4 Discharging the steel

The steel was emptied. To make mild steel, small quantities of carbon and manganese were added.

This liquid steel could be cast immediately into girders or rails – or any shape – without having to be forged like bar iron. Bessemer made a fortune from his process. His works produced steel at around £5 a tonne, compared with normal prices of about £50 a tonne.

This steel had a major impact on engineering and metalwork industries such as weapon-making, machine-tool cutting, wire ropes, shipbuilding and railways.

A Bessemer converter at work, about 1880 ▶

43	Edinburgh	$12\frac{1}{4}$
24	Liverpool	$6\frac{1}{2}$
18	Exeter	$4\frac{3}{4}$
11	Birmingham	3
6	Brighton	$1\frac{1}{4}$
1836	Journey times from London (in hours)	1850

Full steam ahead

Although sailing ships had managed to put up a strong resistance to steamships, horse-drawn coaches could not compete against steam locomotives. Coach companies went out of business, turnpike trusts went bankrupt and the last coach left London in 1846.

What happened to the horses?

These were used to pull cabs and buses, particularly to stations, but their use in towns dropped. Doncaster had 258 horses in 1839 and only 60 in 1845.

▲ The railway network, 1852

By 1850 trains were three times as fast as coaches, with fast express trains reaching 65 km per hour. Trains were eight times faster than canal barges and could carry twenty times as much freight. Canals were, in fact, cheaper for goods traffic, so their decline was slower, but by 1890 they too were struggling to survive.

By 1852 the main-line structure of the railways was in place, and after that most new routes were branch lines. As the government felt it was not its business to interfere in economic affairs, not all lines were sensibly planned, particularly during the years 1844–1847, when a 'railway mania' occurred. Money was poured into 626 new companies, but unrealistic schemes meant that thousands lost their savings.

▲ First-, second- and third-class travel to Epsom Races, 1847

Was train travel cheaper than coach?

Yes, and an Act of 1844 ensured that one train a day ran in each direction, stopping at every station and charging not more than a penny a mile.

This increased what was now called third-class travel, and opened up opportunities for work.

Fish and chips

Railways created work too, and all branches of industry benefited. Iron and steel were needed for locomotives, rails, trucks, signals and buildings. It has been estimated that rails alone took 15% of all iron output in the 1840s.

Bricks were needed for cuttings, bridges and buildings. Timber was needed for sleepers and carriages. Coal was needed for locomotives: a journey of 160 km used one tonne of coal.

Apart from navvies, were other workers needed?

Yes – men to work on the line, in repair sheds, at depots, as guards and so forth. By 1890, 300,000 jobs were connected directly and indirectly to the railways.

New 'railway towns' such as Swindon and Crewe grew up. Crewe's population increased from 203 in 1841 to 18,000 by 1871.

The food industry expanded because of the railways. Fresh food such as milk, meat and fish travelled further. Fish and chips began to replace pig's trotters as a cheap supper.

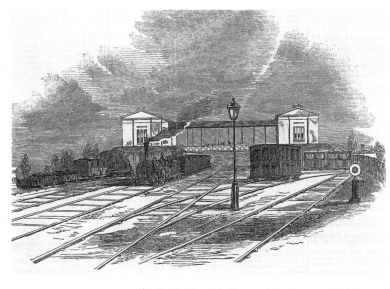

▲ Swindon Railway Station in 1845

The publishing industry also flourished. Trains carried not just letters, but books and newspapers. Every morning people read the same news stories. Every morning they told the same time. Before the railways, clocks in Reading were four minutes later than London's, and those in Bridgwater fourteen minutes later! Everyone adopted Greenwich Mean Time and timetables made sense.

Seaside resorts grew up as a direct consequence of the railways. Some people could afford annual holidays, and working families could enjoy cheap-day excursions. Those born and bred in the town could glimpse the countryside for the first time.

▲ London to Brighton in two hours: day return, 3s 6d

Death of William IV	Queen Victoria comes to the throne	Joseph Paxton: designs Great Exhibition	Crystal Palace: Pre-fabricated glass, steel framework, cast-iron girders	Elm trees in Hyde Park contained under glass	Profits of £186,437 built Victoria and Albert Museum, Science and Natural History Museums, Royal Albert Hall and others
1837		1851 May 1			

The Great Exhibition

Many people bought cheap-day excursion tickets to travel by train for the first time to visit the Great Exhibition of 1851. This was designed to display the 'Works of Industry of all Nations', but it was chiefly a showplace for British manufacturers. As the workshop of the world, Britain was, at this time, at the height of her industrial power. The Exhibition was therefore a celebration of Britain, her empire and of the reign of Queen Victoria.

The Exhibition building itself was one of the wonders of the Industrial Revolution. Rising like a cathedral of glass, it was christened 'Crystal Palace' by the press. Inside there were over 100,000 exhibits. Most were from Britain and her colonies, and the rest were from thirty-nine foreign countries. They included raw materials, machines and handicrafts, and represented the old and the new.

▲ Queen Victoria opens the Great Exhibition, May 1 1851

Prince Albert, the Queen's husband, played a major part in planning the Exhibition, which was designed to honour 'the working bees of the world's hive'. The Prince was keen to promote the themes of work and world peace.

Was the Exhibition popular?

Immensely, if you consider that out of a population of eighteen million in England and Wales, it attracted over six million visitors.

▲ Furniture on display at the Great Exhibition

As well as marvelling at the quality of British manufactured goods, agricultural machinery from America and industrial diamonds from Germany were also admired. Delegates from these and other countries were keen to study Britain's technological innovations.

Africa: Cape Town Railway	India: Great Indian Peninsular Railway	Australia: Victoria and New South Wales Railway	Argentina: Great Southern Railway, Buenos Aires	Japan: Imperial Railways	Denmark, Holland, Italy, Norway, Egypt, Russia	China

1860s and **1870s** Countries in Stephenson's order book   **1882**

Railways and the world

▲ The fitting shop of Stephenson's Locomotive Manufactory, 1864

The railway was a major gift that Britain gave to the world. A newspaper article of 1864 claimed that 'no discovery since the invention of printing had exercised so great a change and produced such remarkable and beneficial results for the whole human race'.

The manufacture of railways was ample proof of Britain's dominance in world trade. In Stephenson's Locomotive Manufactory in Newcastle upon Tyne, a new engine and tender were completed every week. Highly skilled men assembled the locomotives from components made in other parts of the works.

By 1864 the firm was in the hands of a third member of the family, George Robert, a nephew of the original George Stephenson.

Where were the locomotives shipped to?

All round the globe. The firm's order book reflects the demand from different continents.

Unlike Britain, whose railway planning was haphazard, other countries, such as France and the area which became Germany in 1871, planned their railways precisely. They wanted them openly for military purposes.

British materials, equipment, capital and often contractors helped to turn Germany and America into major industrial economies, soon to be compared to Britain's. British contractors would work in a country initially and, once they had trained key staff, those people would take over the building and the maintenance.

Railways helped to spread football too! Contractors and workmen would organise teams to play during breaks.

Railways also produced some exceptional architecture at home and abroad. This rather grandiose station (right) was built in Bombay, India, in 1897.

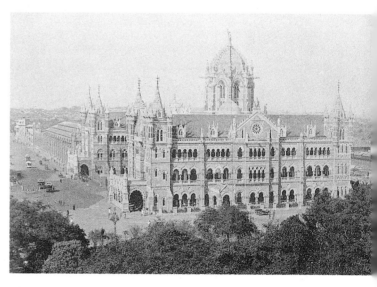

▲ The Victoria Railway Terminus, Bombay

	Birmingham	Bradford	Glasgow	Liverpool	London
1801	71,000	17,000	77,000	82,000	957,000
1851	233,000	104,000	345,000	376,000	2,362,000

Population growth

A glass of sewage

PUBLIC **21** HEALTH

Ten years after the Great Exhibition, Prince Albert died of typhoid, aged forty-two.

What is typhoid?

A disease spread in infected water.

Prince Albert would no doubt at times have drunk water from the same source as John in the poem (right) – the River Thames. Although the Prince had praised the 'working bees', the fact was that less than a stone's throw from the Crystal Palace, thousands of workers were living in over-crowded and insanitary conditions.

The population in towns had grown so rapidly during the Industrial Revolution that insufficient thought had been given to services such as rubbish collection and sewage disposal. As a result ashes, garbage, slaughterhouse waste and sewage was left in backyards, piled in streets or thrown into open channel-drains which ran down streets.

The drains and sewage pipes, if any, ran into local rivers. These rivers often supplied the water for drinking, cooking and washing. Water companies provided most town water, but as this was sometimes taken straight from rivers and untreated, what they supplied was virtually undiluted sewage.

Many people collected their water from communal taps, sometimes shared with hundreds of others. Supplies might be turned on for only a few minutes a day. Others collected rainwater in tubs, black from the residue of smoke from fires and left to become stagnant. Some used wells with pumps over them. These could be contaminated by water seeping into them from cesspits and overcrowded graveyards.

The stench from the Thames was so strong that the windows of the Commons were closed during debates.

THE WATER THAT JOHN DRINKS.

This is the water that JOHN drinks.

This is the Thames with its cento of stink,
That supplies the water that JOHN drinks.

These are the fish that float in the ink-
-y stream of the Thames with its cento of stink,
That supplies the water that JOHN drinks.

This is the sewer, from cesspool and sink,
That feeds the fish that float in the ink-
-y stream of the Thames with its cento of stink,
That supplies the water that JOHN drinks.

▲ A poem from *Punch* magazine, 1849

Housing

▲ A London slum, 1853

What about housing?

Not only did the rivers that flowed through the towns stink, so did many of the houses and their inhabitants.

Houses to accommodate workers were built quickly and often shoddily and cheaply. To save space, they were built in long terraces, or 'back to back'. Others were built around courtyards. Courts could be as little as two metres wide, with a lavatory at one end and the water pump near the other. Ventilation and lighting were inadequate, and as there were no damp courses, moisture spread up the walls, turning them black.

The poorest – who could not afford to rent a house, or two rooms – crammed together in single rooms. Four or five families could live in one room.

Not all slept in beds. Some slept in packing cases or on bundles of straw with sacking for a blanket. Outside lavatories, or privies, were wooden shacks built over an earth closet with a cesspit underneath. As the landlord had to pay for these to be emptied by 'night-men', they were often left to overflow.

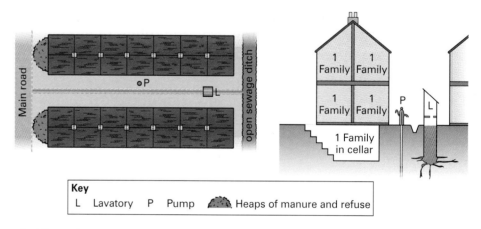

Key
L   Lavatory   P   Pump   Heaps of manure and refuse

▲ Plan of court and 'back to back' housing

The overflow from cesspits and drains could drip down steps to cellars, or ooze up through the cellar floors. Rats, flies, vermin and lice all spread disease. Epidemics spread swiftly in these conditions, especially when malnutrition was commonplace. Typhoid, typhus, diphtheria, scarlet fever, measles and tuberculosis led to high death rates.

In 1831 these were joined by a frightening new disease.

	Bolton	Leeds	Liverpool	Manchester
Labourers	18 years	19 years	15 years	17 years
Gentlemen	34 years	44 years	35 years	38 years

c. 1840   Average age of death

Cholera

By 1831 cholera had spread from Asia and entered Britain through the port of Sunderland. Within months, 32,000 people across the country had died of it.

Nearly half who caught the disease (with its symptoms of cramp, diarrhoea and vomiting) died, most within thirty-six hours or less. Rich and poor alike were affected, but it struck hardest in the poorest overcrowded areas. The government set up a Central Board of Health and encouraged towns to set up local Boards of Health.

These tried to defeat cholera by several measures, which included providing lime to whitewash houses, and burning barrels of tar and vinegar to disinfect the streets and disperse the smell. It was thought that fumes from dung, sewers, graveyards or crowded rooms contained 'miasma', a poisonous matter in the air which caused diseases.

One firm believer in this miasmatic theory of disease was Edwin Chadwick, the Secretary of the Poor Law Commission and a tireless reformer. In 1842 he published a report which revealed the grim living conditions of the poor. He argued that Parliament should take responsibility for public health, but there was a general reluctance to accept his recommendations.

▲ Burning tar in Exeter, 1832

▲ Washing the bedclothes of the deceased in the stream providing the water supply, Exeter, 1832

Why?

The government felt that it should have nothing to do with cleanliness. They thought it was better to let people sort out problems themselves rather than spend revenue from taxes on improvements for the benefit of all.

This attitude of *laissez-faire* ('leave well alone') persisted until the next outbreak of cholera in 1848.

	Cholera			Chadwick's 'Report on the Sanitary Condition of the Labouring Population'	Public Health Act: Central Board in London Local Boards to oversee services such as sewerage	Louis Pasteur: Germ theory of disease
32,000 deaths	62,000 deaths	20,000 deaths	14,000 deaths			
	Miasmatic theory of disease					
1831	1848	1854	1866	1842	1848	1865

Sewers at last

The 1848 outbreak of cholera killed 62,000 people. It prompted the government to pass a Public Health Act. It had the powers to set up local Boards of Health when the death rate reached 23 per 1,000 people, but yet again nothing was compulsory. As before, few towns undertook initiatives, and when the Board of Health was disbanded six years later, only a sixth of the population was served by local boards.

Opposition to parliamentary interference continued. *The Times* newspaper called the 1848 Act 'a reckless invasion of property and liberty'.

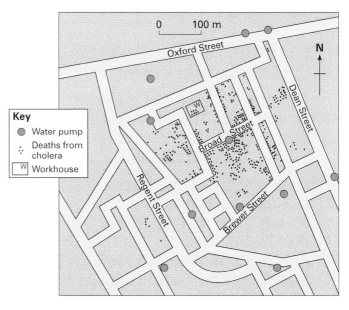

▲ Map of cholera epidemic, Soho, 1854

Individuals continued to take further action, however. In 1848 the first medical officer of health for London, Dr John Simon, set out to provide a pure, filtered water supply and began a medical inspection of houses. In 1854 Dr John Snow investigated cases of cholera in Soho.

What did he find?

He found that people in the workhouse, with their own well, were mostly free of the disease. No one from the local brewery took ill. Most deaths occurred in those who drew water from the Broad Street pump. Dr Snow removed the pump handle and the number of deaths from sewage-infected water in Soho declined.

▲ Building the sewers

In 1858 the stench from the Thames was so bad that Parliament had to suspend sittings. Parliament rushed through a Bill giving a Metropolitan Board, created in 1855, more powers. The Board's chief engineer, Joseph Bazalgette, could put into effect his plans to build sewers. By 1865 eighty-three miles of sewers had been built, discharging up to 420 million gallons a day at Barking and Plumstead.

Municipal Corporations Act: Creation of town councils elected by ratepayers	Vote extended to all male householders in towns	Public Health Act: Amended and consolidated earlier acts Enforced drainage, sanitation and water supplies	All authorities to employ health inspectors
1835	1867	1875	

The 'city fathers'

As the nineteenth century progressed, it became clearer that the government's policy of *laissez-faire* was not solving the problems of cities.

A Municipal Corporations Act of 1835 had set up 178 new corporations (town councils) in cities and towns. As their powers increased, they used money raised from local taxes to improve their respective environments. Many towns spent heavily on sewers, drainage and water supply.

In was in 1875 that the government made itself responsible for large-scale improvements. The Conservatives under Disraeli passed a Public Health Act which set up a nationwide system of sanitary authorities. These were given wider powers to enforce drainage, sanitation and water supplies. The average life expectancy increased by ten years between 1850 and 1900.

▲ Terraced housing in Manchester, built in the late nineteenth century

Did housing improve?

Laws were passed which stated that houses had to be a certain distance apart and courtyards open at one end.

▲ Leeds Town Hall

In 1875 an Artisans' and Labourers' Dwelling Act permitted councils to take over and clear slum districts. Joseph Chamberlain, Mayor of Birmingham, demolished 16 hectares of slums near the city centre. In his own words, he 'parked, paved, assized, marketed, gas and watered and improved'.

Many town councillors, who became known as 'city fathers', encouraged initiatives. Municipal baths and wash-houses were opened. Cemeteries were laid out properly, and municipal parks with flowerbeds, bandstands and boating lakes graced cities. Libraries, art galleries, concert halls and splendid town halls became common. People began to take pride in their towns and cities.

UNIONS

22

Skilled workers

Despite parliamentary legislation to improve public health, housing and working conditions, standards of living varied greatly. Skilled workers were helped by the setting up of 'new model unions' in the 1850s and 1860s.

What kind of organisations were they?

Although these nationally organised unions were not completely against strikes, they tried not to confront employers but to work with them. The emphasis was on negotiation rather than strike action.

▲ Union membership certificate of the Amalgamated Society of Engineers

The first of these, the Amalgamated Society of Engineers (ASE), set up in 1851, joined together over a hundred local trade societies of millwrights, machinists, engineers and tool-makers. In return for a high entrance fee and subscription, members received benefits during illness, unemployment and old age. By 1860 the ASE had 21,000 members. Several other national craft unions followed.

The ASE membership certificate (left) shows Mars the God of War being rejected, but there were still unions prepared to use violence. In 1866 unionists in the Sheffield cutlery trade attacked the homes of 'blacklegs' (workers who refused to join the union) and murdered one man.

A Royal Commission of Enquiry of 1867 decided that this action was exceptional and that most unions were peaceful organisations. This decision helped the passing of the Trades Union Act of 1871 which gave unions legal protection. In the same year another Act made picketing (preventing anyone from entering a workplace) illegal.

By this time union representatives from many trades had formed a Trades Union Congress (TUC). In the 1874 general election the TUC advised members to vote against the Liberals who had prevented picketing. When the Tories were elected, they passed an Act which made picketing legal. Unions grew in strength again.

Match girls' Strike: 6.30 am–6 pm, standing all day $\frac{1}{2}$ d an hour for dangerous work of dipping matches in phosphorus	Gasworkers' Strike: 12 hours a day shovelling coal	Dockers' Strike: Casual labour paid by hour	Seamstresses, domestic workers and shop workers not protected by Factory Acts
1888	1889	1889	

Semi-skilled and unskilled workers

Did these workers have unions too?

Apart from the miners and agricultural workers, the poorer workers had not organised themselves.

What strengthened the unions was a number of successful London strikes in the years 1888 and 1889. These included a strike by female workers at the Bryant and May match factory in the East End of London. Helped by Annie Besant, a journalist who won support for them through newspaper articles, the women won better working conditions within three weeks.

In 1889 the gas workers, led by Will Thorne, won a reduction from a twelve-hour to an eight-hour working day. The London dockers attracted a great deal of public sympathy. As casual labourers, they had no job security and went on strike for four hours' continuous work at one time and a minimum of 6d (the 'dockers' tanner') an hour. With funds from unions, money from the public, takings at football matches and £30,000 from Australian trade unionists and sympathisers, they succeeded.

▲ Match girls in a protest march to Westminster

▲ A family living in one room in the 1890s

These strikes inspired the formation of other powerful unions such as the Miners' Federation of Great Britain, but the employers fought back. They joined together and employed 'blackleg' labour. The gas workers lost a strike in 1890 and the Dockers' Union, formed after their strike, collapsed in 1891. Once again workers turned to Parliament.

After the 1884 election, there were eleven working-class MPs in Parliament, known as 'Labour' or 'Lib-Labs' as they sat with the Liberals in the Commons. Now many workers pushed for the setting up of a separate workers' political party to push through social reforms to stamp out poverty.

Emigration from:	1815–1834	1835–1860	1861–1880	1881–1900	Totals
England and Wales	100,000	1,000,000	1,600,000	3,000,000	5,700,000
Ireland	400,000	2,600,000	1,400,000	1,300,000	5,700,000
Scotland	30,000	250,000	300,000	500,000	1,080,000

Emigration

One escape route from the drudgery of poverty in the nineteenth century was emigration. Between 1815 and 1900, 13 million people left Britain to seek a better life, chiefly in America, but increasingly in Canada, Australia and New Zealand.

▲ A last look at England

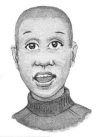

How could people afford the fare?

The government, which wanted British people to live in Australia and New Zealand, offered free passages.

The Poor Law Commission financed the departure of over 14,000 people from Norfolk alone between 1836 and 1846. Both the government and the commission advertised for workers such as shepherds, miners, agricultural labourers and domestic servants of 'good character'. Single women between eighteen and thirty were particularly in demand.

Landlords, who found the cost of the poor rate burdensome, paid the fare of farmworkers. Religious groups such as the Salvation Army, founded in 1876, helped paupers to emigrate.

Not all emigrants were forced out by poverty, however. Many welcomed the prospect of cheap farming land, a steady job, higher wages and better living conditions. The discovery of gold in California (1849), Australia (1851), the Transvaal, Africa (1880) and in the Klondike, Alaska (1890s) tempted those who hoped to make a fortune.

Early trade unionists and Chartists emigrated after the setbacks in their movements, and the new trade unions kept an emigration fund to help members finance their passage. Travel by rail and steamship, which became quicker and safer, encouraged people to leave.

▲ The postal system brought news of relatives who had emigrated. In this painting the man is holding a letter and a map of Australia

 **Insect eater:** Long beak for picking insects out of tree trunks and branches

 Seed eater: Strong, crushing beak for picking seeds off the ground

Vegetarian finch: Strong beak for eating buds and leaves

 **Insect eater:** Strong, sharp beak for grabbing and cutting

Four of the thirteen Galapagos finches

A revolution in evolution

As the emigrants settled into their new environments, they adapted to changes in climate, soil, crops and cultures. Many intermarried and became American or Australian, rather than Welsh or English.

In 1859 Charles Darwin, son of Erasmus Darwin, suggested in his book *The Origin of Species* that all species change through natural selection – the preservation of those species best suited to survive. He suggested that life had not been created but had evolved.

Was this controversial?

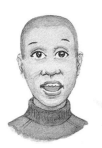

Extremely, as belief in the Bible's creation story was widespread.

To most people God had created the world and every species in it, and these species remained exactly the same as when God created them. The fossils dug from canals that Erasmus Darwin had studied were thought to be remains of creatures destroyed by the Great Flood in the Noah's Ark story.

Darwin's theory of evolution was not new, but he backed up his findings with scientific evidence, including fossils collected from his five-year voyage as an amateur naturalist to the South Atlantic and then the Pacific. One of many fascinating observations he made was that finches on separate Galapagos Islands had developed different beaks. They had survived because they had adapted to their different environments.

Later, in 1872, Darwin published *The Descent of Man*, in which he suggested that man and apes are descended from a common ancestor. By the time of his death in 1882, the Church, scientists and the public had become reconciled, some uneasily, to the idea of evolution. This revolutionary thinker of the nineteenth century was buried in Westminster Abbey alongside a revolutionary thinker of the eighteenth century, Sir Isaac Newton.

▲ Darwin and 'friend'

Mob burn down new telegraph office at Barrackpore	Rising at Meerut garrison	Delhi taken, other risings	45,000 British and 232,000 Indian troops	Cawnpore massacre	Delhi retaken	Agra retaken	Lucknow retaken
1857 January	May 10	May 11		June	September	October	**1858** March

The British Raj

Indians felt that the British Raj ('rule') had made too many changes which disturbed their ancient practices and beliefs. Railways, for example, were distrusted because it meant that Indians of different castes were obliged to travel together. India had 2,000 castes connected to their religions, and these defined people socially according to their jobs and breeding. Higher and lower castes never mingled.

The banning of suttee – the burning alive of a Hindu widow alongside the corpse of her husband, a custom some Indians wanted retained – was particularly resented.

The Indians also suspected the British were trying to introduce Christianity, especially through the missionary schools where every lesson was taught in English.

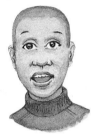

How did these grievances turn to violence?

There was a religious blunder over the greasing of gun cartridges.

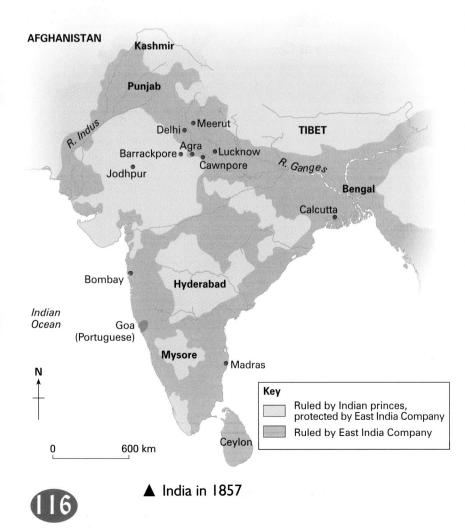

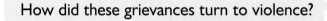

▲ India in 1857

A new Enfield rifle had been developed for general use. As before, the sepoys (Indian soldiers) had to bite the top from the cartridge and ease it down the muzzle to load the gun. The new rifles worked better when cartridges were greased with tallow and animal fats rather than with vegetable oil and wax as previously.

British suppliers had been warned that Hindus were forbidden to touch beef fat and Muslims pork fat. When production began in India, no definite instructions were given. Rumours that pork and beef fat had been used spread like wildfire through the garrisons. At Meerut, north of Delhi, sepoys of the Bengal army rejected the guns. Eighty-five were stripped of their uniform and gaoled for ten years for insubordination. One cavalry and three infantry regiments spontaneously rebelled, murdering several officers and their families. They then fled to Delhi and seized the city, murdering every European there.

British Government of India Act	East India Company ended	Viceroy answerable only to monarch	62,000 British troops, 125,000 Indian troops wear Queen's colours	Queen Victoria made Empress of India	Only 5% of senior posts in Civil Service filled by Indians
1858 November			**1863**	**1877**	**1914**

The Indian Mutiny

The British now faced a mutiny, a civil war involving her own soldiers.

Did all the sepoys take part?

No. Thousands, including Ghurkas, the Sikhs and the Pathan regiments, remained loyal to the Raj.

The mutineers converged on three garrisons at Agra, Lucknow and Cawnpore where the British had withdrawn. Under the leadership of Nana Sahib, a prince, the mutineers laid siege to a thousand men, women and children at Cawnpore. After two weeks, Nana Sahib offered the remaining few hundred left alive a safe passage. As they boarded the waiting boats, they were callously butchered. Within two weeks the 125 survivors of this massacre, all women and children, were murdered.

Revenge by the British on the mutineers was equally horrific. By forcing pork and beef fat down the sepoys' throats, their caste was broken and their damnation was ensured following a gruesome death.

The mutiny was crushed, but the British were taken aback by the ferocity of feeling that had been shown against them. The immediate result was the takeover of the powers of the East India Company and the government of India by Parliament in London. Local laws and policy-making were undertaken by a viceroy and provincial governor-generals, assisted by councils who included some Indian princes.

The Indian civil service was reformed and entrance was by examination so Indians could apply. The Indian army was reorganised to allow Indians to take positions of command. By 1900 the Indians had been granted a small share in government, but to educated Indians this was soon to be regarded as insufficient.

▲ Massacre at Cawnpore, 1857

▲ Lucknow is recaptured, 1858

117

Dominion of Canada: 4 provinces	Australia: 6 self-governing colonies	Commonwealth (dominion) of Australia	New Zealand: British take possession	Disputes with Maoris over land	Dominion of New Zealand: Internal self-government, Britain controls defence and foreign affairs
1867	1855	1901 January 1	1840	1852	1907

The dominions

What were the dominions?

These were Britain's colonies of settlements which became self-governing.

The first colonies to be granted dominion status were those in Canada. There had been minor riots in both upper Canada (Ontario) where British settlers lived, and in lower Canada (Quebec) where descendants of the original French settlers lived. In a report of 1839, Lord Durham, who had been sent to investigate the causes of unrest, suggested that the colonies should be united and that Canadians should be given responsibility for their own affairs.

Key
Original provinces of the Dominion of Canada established 1867 by the British North America Act

Dominion of Canada 1912

Canadian Pacific Railway 1885

▲ The dominion of Canada

In 1867 each colony – Quebec, Ontario, New Brunswick and Nova Scotia – was made a province. These formed a dominion, with a central government at Ottawa. British Columbia agreed to join the dominion if a railway was built to link it with the east. The Canadian Pacific Railway, nearly 5,000 kilometres long, helped to unite Canada.

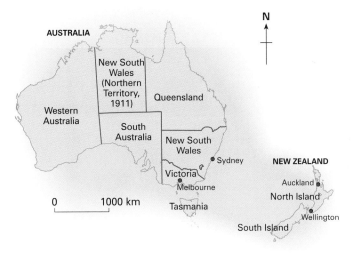

By the 1890s the six separate colonies of Australia sought some form of unity but none of the colonies was willing to give up its own independence. A federal government, in which a central government shares power with regional governments but is responsible for national concerns such as defence, was decided upon, and Australia became a dominion on January 1 1901. New Zealand became the third self-governing dominion in 1907.

The dominions maintained close and co-operative relations with Britain. Queen Victoria remained the head of state and her features were printed on postage stamps and coins.

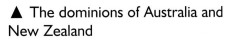

▲ The dominions of Australia and New Zealand

Home Government Association	Irish Home Rule League	59 Home Rule MPs	Splits in party	Parnell leads Home Rule Party	Parnell forms Irish National League	Irish Loyal and Patriotic Union	Irish Unionist Party
1870 May	1873 November	1874	1878–1879	1880	1882	1885	1886

Ireland and Home Rule

Many people in Ireland, including the Fenians, wanted Ireland to become self-governing. This demand for home government, or Home Rule, became popular and in 1873 a Home Rule League (Party) was set up, with fifty-nine MPs elected in 1874.

After several disputes and changes in leadership, Charles Stewart Parnell, leader of the Irish Parliamentary Party in Westminster, set up a new Irish National League in which Home Rule was first priority. The Protestants in Ireland became alarmed as the Catholic Church supported the League. Protestants in Ireland, known as Unionists (as they supported the Act of Union of 1801), did not want Home Rule in Ireland. They feared that if it was successful, Catholics would be in the majority, and they preferred to belong to the United Kingdom with its Protestant majority.

Protestants in the North, the Ulster Unionists, were a mixture of Presbyterian Scots by ancestry and Anglicans. They buried their differences to support the Union. They were worried that the prosperity of Belfast, which had many trade links with Britain, would suffer if Ireland became independent.

The Orange Order, too, supported the Union.

What was the Orange Order?

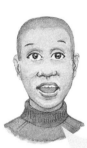

The Orange Order was founded in the 1790s, about a hundred years after the Battle of the Boyne when William of Orange defeated the Catholics. Its purpose was to uphold the Protestant constitution and monarch of the United Kingdom.

Using the colour orange to represent Protestantism, the Orange Order organised demonstrations, including annual marches associated with Protestant victories over Catholics. It gave the Ulster Protestants a sense of unity.

There were fewer Protestants in the south, but as the Home Rule movement gained momentum they formed, in 1885, the Irish Loyal and Patriotic Union.

▲ Unionist demonstration, Belfast

First Home Rule Bill	Defeat of Home Rule Bill	Conservatives in power: No Home Rule	Home Rule Party voice of Irish Catholics	Unionist Party replaces Conservatives and Liberals in Ireland: voice of Irish Protestants	Second Home Rule Bill defeated in Lords	Gladstone retires
1886 April	June		1886	1886	1893	1894

The Home Rule Bill

The Prime Minister in Britain who supported Home Rule for Ireland was William Ewart Gladstone of the Liberal Party. He was keen to remove Irish grievances and had already tried to tackle both church and land issues. In April 1886, after discussion with Irish Liberal MPs, he introduced his Home Rule Bill to the Commons. It proposed that:

- Ireland should have its own Parliament in Dublin, consisting of two Houses.

- This Parliament should elect the Irish government.

- It would deal with all Irish affairs but not the Crown, defence, war and peace, trade and navigation, coinage, the post office and colonial relations.

- There would be no Irish MPs in Westminster.

- Ireland would pay one-fifteenth of the imperial budget.

Was the Bill accepted?

There was a lot of hostility against it in Britain.

▲ Parliament rejects Gladstone's Home Rule Bill

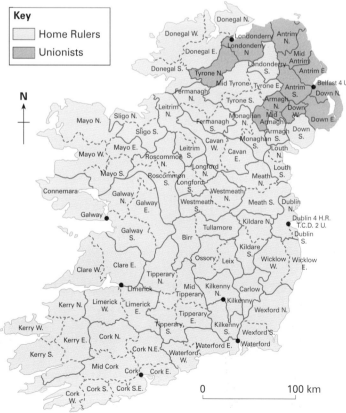

Many Protestants supported the Irish Unionists because they were fellow-Protestants. They feared that if Ireland became independent it might support enemies of Britain. They thought the unity of the empire would be weakened and that Anglo-Irish trade would diminish. Many had a racist view of the Irish and felt they were not capable of ruling themselves.

Not all of Gladstone's party supported him. These were called the Liberal Unionists. On June 8 1886, ninety-three members of Gladstone's party voted against the Bill. Gladstone called a general election. In Ireland the Home Rule Party won eighty-five seats to the Unionists' eighteen. In Britain, however, the Conservatives and Liberal Unionists won by a clear majority.

Gladstone resigned. When he made a second attempt to introduce the Bill in 1893 and was defeated, Gladstone was forced to retire.

Key
- Home Rulers
- Unionists

▲ Results of the 1886 general election in Ireland

We don't want to fight,
But by Jingo if we do,
We've got the ships,
We've got the men,
We've got the money too.

1890s music hall song

C is for colonies,
Rightly we boast,
That of all the great nations,
Great Britain has the most!

1899 'ABC for Baby Patriots': nursery book rhyme

THE BRITISH EMPIRE
26
AFTER 1890

Jubilee and jingoism

Troops from every part of the empire marched through London to celebrate Queen Victoria's Diamond Jubilee in 1897. Although Britain was no longer the only 'workshop of the world', and other nations such as America and Germany were becoming increasingly industrialised, she still controlled the largest empire.

Pride in belonging to such an imperial country was at its height. It was demonstrated by this show of loyalty to the Queen and a sense of 'doing one's duty for the country'. Patriotic pride was encouraged in books and newspapers.

Magazines for boys were called *Chums, Pluck, Young England* and *Union Jack*. War correspondents in new, cheaper newspapers wrote vivid accounts of imperial campaigns. The spread of the telegraph network meant that news of any battle could reach Britain in twenty-four hours.

▲ Jubilee celebration plate

What effect did this have?

During the Boer War in Africa, people crowded into fairgrounds and music halls to see newsreel films from the battle front, shown on the newly invented cinematograph, and cheered at victories.

The music hall gave birth to a popular song, which added a new word, 'jingoism', to the English language (see above). Because the British people seemed to have spread across the globe and mastered each environment, some patriots felt that they belonged to a superior nation, a super-race. Any insult to the nation was met with swaggering aggression.

When the army suffered a series of humiliating defeats in Africa, however, many people at home and abroad began to realise that the British were no longer invincible.

▲ Middle-class boys in sailor suits, playing with toy cannon and lead soldiers

South Africa

Who was Britain fighting in Africa?

Not the Africans, but the Afrikaners, or Boers. These were white settlers, farmers of Dutch and French ancestry, who had settled in the Cape of Good Hope in 1652. As Calvinists they believed that the land and their 25,000 black slaves had been willed to them by God.

In 1815 Britain acquired the Cape from the Dutch during the Napoleonic Wars. After 1833, when slavery in the empire was abolished, the Boers moved into the hinterland on a Great Trek which lasted several years. There they set up two independent states, later called Transvaal and Orange Free State. In 1886 the discovery of gold in the Transvaal transformed the economy. Thousands of settlers, known as Uitlanders ('foreign workers'), moved there.

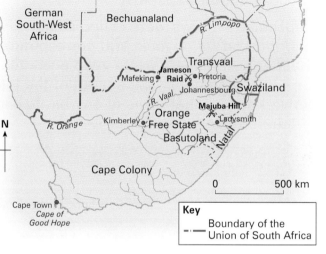

▲ South Africa

By this time Britain's empire in Africa had expanded considerably. In 1884, after a conference of European powers, Africa had been divided up between these powers; Britain gained further colonies in the east and west. The premier of Cape Colony, Cecil Rhodes, had immense personal ambitions to link Britain's empire from the Cape to Cairo. He encouraged the British Uitlanders in the Transvaal to rebel and overthrow the leader, Paul Kruger. He offered the support of his private army, led by a Dr Jameson.

The Uitlanders failed to rise, and Jameson's raid with 470 troops was easily overpowered when the soldiers crossed into the Transvaal. Relationships between Kruger and Britain continued to deteriorate. When Britain refused to withdraw troops from the Boer frontier, war broke out.

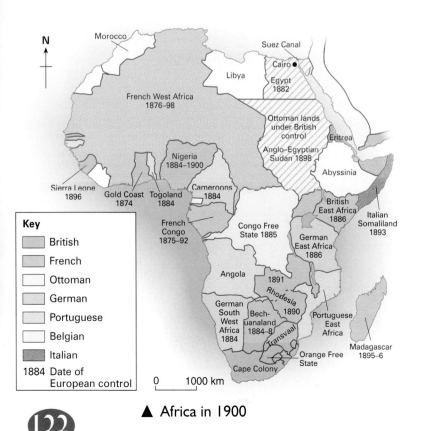

▲ Africa in 1900

British arrive at Pretoria, Transvaal	Last Boer army defeated	First use of term 'concentration camp'	Peace of Vereeniging	450,000 British troops took 3 years to defeat 50,000 Boers	Transvaal and Orange Free State self-governing	Union of South Africa
1900 June	August		**1902**		**1907**	**1910**

The Boer War

When war broke out in 1899 the Boers besieged the British at Ladysmith (Natal), Kimberley (Cape Colony) and Mafeking (Bechuanaland). The British were stunned when their troops were defeated in battle attempting to relieve Ladysmith and Kimberley. They had underestimated the Boers, who were skilled fighters – mobile, adept at bushcraft and armed with modern rifles and artillery. Only by reinforcing the army and using new strategies did the British eventually relieve the three garrisons and reach Pretoria in the Transvaal.

▲ Troops leaving Southampton to fight in the Boer War

Although the last Boer army had now been defeated, Kruger refused to surrender. His younger commanders conducted successful guerrilla warfare, with raids on camps and communication lines. Then Kitchener, the British commander, launched counter-strategies which included destroying farms and livestock and crowding Boer women, children and their black servants into concentration camps. Out of 116,000 people 'concentrated' into camps, 28,000 (mostly children) died, chiefly of epidemic diseases.

Wasn't this policy of concentration camps controversial?

Yes, many people around the world were shocked at the brutality of the British.

By 1902, when both sides were exhausted, peace negotiations began. The British regained political supremacy but the Boers were promised restored self-government in the Transvaal and Orange Free State.

In this, her largest imperialist war, Britain had mobilised 450,000 soldiers, including 55,000 from the colonies. 4,000 Boers lost their lives, 7,792 British empire troops died fighting and a further 13,000 died from illness. The war had shown how determined Britain was to retain global power, whatever the cost. Some British people lost their enthusiasm for the empire when they counted this cost.

▲ The young Winston Churchill as a war correspondent

ASIA	AMERICA	AFRICA	AUSTRALASIA
Ceylon, India, Singapore, Hong Kong, Malaya	Canada, Bermuda, Bahamas, Barbados, Jamaica, Leeward Islands, Falklands Islands, British Guiana	South Africa, Rhodesia, Kenya, Uganda, Sudan, Nigeria, Gambia, Gold Coast, Nyasaland, Sierra Leone	Australia, New Zealand, Fiji

1901 Principal colonies in four continents

End of an era

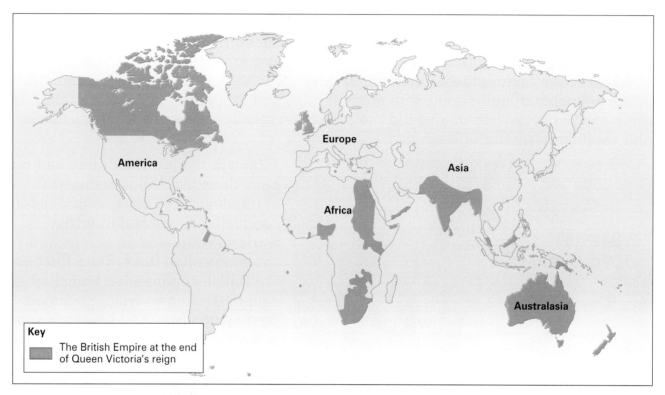

Key
The British Empire at the end of Queen Victoria's reign

▲ The British empire, 1901

By the time of Queen Victoria's death in 1901, Britain's empire was still the largest in the world, with countries in every continent and islands in every ocean. As it covered both the hemispheres, it was known as 'the empire on which the sun never sets'.

▲ The Dreadnought battleship

Despite the wealth that trade with her empire generated, however, Britain began to fall behind some industrialised countries. The Germans developed a chemical industry which began to lead the world. The USA leapt ahead in the making of machines such as the typewriter, the sewing machine and the Colt revolver, for which there was a vast demand. It also manufactured the motor car, chiefly a French and German invention.

Britain still dominated the world's shipbuilding industry and her navy remained powerful, although French and German warships also cruised regularly in the Atlantic, Indian and Pacific Oceans.

She responded to the growing fear of German military shipbuilding by producing the Dreadnought battleship in 1906. Within eight years they were brought into military action. The sun that never sets had been eclipsed by the gathering storm clouds of a terrible world war.

Kings and Queens

Name	Also known as	Age at succession	Family	Died	Buried
William III	William of Orange (before his succession)	Age 38 as King of England and Ireland on February 23, and as King of Scotland on May 11	Wife: Mary Children: None	March 8, Kensington Palace Age 51 Of a broken collarbone sustained when his horse stumbled over a molehill	Westminster Abbey
Born 1650		👑 1689		**Died 1702**	
and Mary II		Age 26 as Queen of England and Ireland on February 23, and as Queen of Scotland on May 11	Husband: William Children: None	Age 32 Of smallpox	King Henry VII's Chapel, Westminster Abbey
Born 1662		👑 1689		**Died 1694**	
Anne	Last monarch of House of Stuart	Age 37 as Queen of England, Scotland and Ireland Age 42 as first titular Queen of Great Britain and Ireland after May 1 1707, the date of the Act of Union	Husband: Prince George of Denmark Children: 17 pregnancies, 5 children born alive but only one, William, survived, dying at 11	August 1, Kensington Palace Age 49 After an apoplectic fit	Westminster Abbey
Born 1665		👑 1702		**Died 1714**	
George I	First monarch of House of Hanover Elector of Hanover	Age 54 as King of Great Britain and Ireland	Wife: Sophia Dorothea Children: GEORGE, Sophia Dorothea	June 12, near Osnabrück Age 67 After a paralytic stroke caused by indigestion from melons eaten when he had not sufficiently recovered from sea-sickness	Osnabrück, Hanover
Born 1660		👑 1714		**Died 1727**	
George II	Elector of Hanover	Age 44 as King of Great Britain and Ireland	Wife: Caroline of Anspach Children: Frederick, Anne, Amelia, Caroline, GEORGE, William, Mary, Louisa	October 25, Kensington Palace Age 76 From a burst blood vessel	Westminster Abbey
Born 1683		👑 1727		**Died 1760**	

Name	Also known as	Age at succession	Family	Died	Buried
George III	Farmer George, Elector of Hanover	Age 22 as King of Great Britain and Ireland	Wife: Charlotte Sophia. Children: GEORGE (Prince Regent), Frederick, WILLIAM (Duke of Clarence), Charlotte, Edward, Augusta, Elizabeth, Ernest, Augustus, Adolphus, Mary, Sophia, Octavius, Alfred, Amelia	January 29, Windsor. Age 81. Of old age and porphyria	St George's Chapel, Windsor
Born 1738		♔ 1760		**Died 1820**	
George IV	Prince Regent (before succession), Prinny, King of Hanover	Age 57 as King of Great Britain and Ireland	Wife 1: Maria Fitzherbert, union not valid according to Royal Marriages Act of 1772. Wife 2: Caroline Amelia Elizabeth. Child of Caroline: Charlotte	June 25, Windsor. Age 67. Of the effect of obesity on the heart, suffering from dropsy, gout, gall stones and blindness, and overdosed with laudanum	St George's Chapel, Windsor
Born 1762		♔ 1820		**Died 1830**	
William IV	The Royal Tar, The Sailor King, King of Hanover	Age 64 as King of Great Britain and Ireland	Wife: Adelaide. Children: Charlotte, Elizabeth	June 20, Windsor. Age 71. Of a circulatory disorder aggravated by asthma	St George's Chapel, Windsor
Born 1765		♔ 1830		**Died 1837**	
Victoria	Last of the Hanoverians. Kingdom of Hanover passed to her uncle Ernest, Duke of Cumberland. Proclaimed Empress of India, 1877	Age 18 as Queen of Great Britain and Ireland	Husband: Albert Prince of Saxe-Coburg-Gotha. Children: Victoria, EDWARD, Alice, Alfred, Helena, Louise, Arthur, Leopold, Beatrice	January 22, Osborne, Isle of Wight. Age 81. Of old age	Frogmore, Windsor
Born 1819		♔ 1837		**Died 1901**	

Index